Laughs and Kixxxx

Jo Adams

IT TAKES ONE TO KNOW ONE

IT TAKES ONE
TO
KNOW ONE

The Joey Adams Do-It-Yourself Laugh Kit

BY JOEY ADAMS

G. P. Putnam's Sons   *New York*

© 1959 BY JOEY ADAMS

Published simultaneously in the Dominion of Canada
by Longmans, Green & Company, Toronto.

Library of Congress Catalog
Card Number: 59-14385

MANUFACTURED IN THE UNITED STATES OF AMERICA

VAN REES PRESS • NEW YORK

TO MY FELLOW COMEDIANS...

Some of my best friends are jokes, and all of my best friends and my best jokes are in this book.

CONTENTS

FOREWORD   9

INTRODUCTION   13

PART ONE

Chapter 1 THE WIT AND THE HUMORIST   19

Chapter 2 THE MURDERERS   24

Chapter 3 THE ANGRY YOUNG MEN   29

Chapter 4 JOKE TELLER, CLOWN AND SATIRIST   38

Chapter 5 IT TAKES ONE TO KNOW ONE   50

PART TWO

Chapter 1 THE ABC OF COMEDY   59

Chapter 2 CREATING THE GAG   64

Chapter 3 THE MONOLOGUE   66
     Alaska   66
     The Martians   68
     Texas   71
     Sex   74
     Russia   80
     Hollywood   86

Chapter 4 THE ADAMS DAILY DOZEN   91

PART THREE

Chapter 1 SOME OF MY BEST FRIENDS ARE JOKES   95

Chapter 2 JOEY'S PORTABLE GAG FILE   103

THE ADAMS APPENDIX   193

FOREWORD

HI. I'm Cindy. Cindy Adams. Better known (to my in-laws, anyway) as Joey Adams' wife. The publishers asked me to say a few kind words about what it's like to live with Joey . . . but I prefer to tell the truth. . . .

My comic husband is one of this planet's foremost comedians, authors and authorities on the subject of humor. I know this because he tells it to me frequently. Joey, who lives, breathes and eats comedy, is a true comedian right down to the marrow of his funny bone. He has one-liners where his veins should be; he has a joke file where his brain should be. He even banks at The Corn Exchange. As someone once said, "Joey is one big joke!"—but who listens to my mother?

No matter what the situation, everything reminds him of a gag. When he was a-courtin' me, he'd whisk me up to his apartment—which was decorated in early scrapbook—turn down the lights, turn up the music, crouch on one creaking knee, and whisper gently, "Will you promise to love, honor and applaud?"

Or when we were walking down the aisle. I was dressed all in bridal white and he was dressed all in TV blue and it was a race as to what was the loudest: ye olde Wedding March or ye old bridegroom. The music and Joey were both playing and 'twas a perfect blending. . . . Tum-tum-tee-tum, "Marriage is like a quiz show. You lose if you give the right answer." Tum-tum-tee-tum, "Nowadays two people can live as cheaply as one large family used to." Tum-tum-tee-tum-tum-tee-tum-tum-tee-tum, "Marriage is give and take and you'd better give it to her or she'll take it anyway."

Mothers, attempting to discover what makes an ordinary, happy, carefree child become a comedian, ask, "Where did he go wrong? Is it because we as parents have failed? How can we detect the early signs?" Adams' case, I figure, began at birth when the MD, doubling as MC, paddled him and the first sound his little pink ears heard was applause. And the first words his little pink ears heard were, "Congratulations on your beautiful delivery." And the first words his enormous pink mouth spoke were not "mummy" or "daddy" but, "A funny thing happened to me on the way to the nursery."

Now that we've been Mr. & Mrs. since February '52 I've noticed he's toned down somewhat or, maybe, eight years of wedded blitz have pitched me higher. . . . Anyway, I no longer deem his strange behavior strange. Living with a human joke machine, if you call that living, is perfectly normal. It seems everybody else is nuts. To me, it's become the norm to wake up, chirp "Good morning, husband, dear" and be answered with, "What's funny about that?" Were he ever to answer my "Good morning" with a "Good morning," I'd worry.

In Chez Adams His Highness bounds out of bed at the crack of 2 P.M. with his usual good humor. Ohhhh, occasionally there are thunderclouds like when our maid uttered the dread words, "I saw Whodoyoucallit on television last night and he was very funny." This caused sulk-itis, the usual cheery disposition went AWOL and he whined, "You know you're not allowed to mention other comedians in this house. Just for that I'll tear all the hairs out of your broom. . . . So, what did he do?"

"Well," she said, "he told a joke. Of course it's not as funny as you are." I wondered how she meant that. She continued, "He told the one about the guy who'd catch sparrows, dip them in iodine and sell 'em as canaries."

"I did that one over ten years ago," Joey squelched as he wrote it down. "Did you hear the one about the girl who was so dumb that when she rented an apartment, the landlady left the 'vacant' sign up?"

"Eddie Cantor did that one over twenty years ago," sneered our *ex*-maid.

Outside of frightening moments like that J.A. is usually good-natured, gay, fun, bright, charming—and he's peering over my shoulder as I write this.

He has a few minor peculiarities . . . nothing really worth mentioning . . . but he does, occasionally, like, f'rinstance, when he's with other humans he'll ofttimes get a faraway look in his eyes, grab a pencil and write furiously. 'Tis then that one knows The Creative Genius' gag-machine brain has just manufactured a ten-minute routine on "politics" or something and has ground to a temporary halt.

Once, when attending a meeting to raise funds for some local charity, I found him grinning happily right through the chairlady's speech, which was designed to wrench a donation out of a miser—that is, the ordinary, common, everyday type miser—not Joey!! He just squatted there grinning and scribbling and his sole contribution was three sock lines on "fund raising."

To some wives, unaccustomed to hardships, Joey Adams mightn't be what you'd call "The Catch of the Year," but to me he's a great writer, a wonderful husband and a terrific comedian. Me, I vote for Joey Adams. . . . But then I voted for Tom Dewey and Adlai Stevenson . . .

CINDY ADAMS

INTRODUCTION

LAUGH and the world laughs with you—but only if the joke is good. If you want to "make funny" for the people you must be prepared for battle. Jokes are a comedian's stock in trade and if you don't have a good stock of jokes, you ain't gonna trade in no laughs.

A plumber can't work without his tools. What is Liberace without his teeth or Brigitte Bardot without her towel? Bob Hope is lost without his passport or take the case of Jayne Mansfield . . .

The dictionary defines a joke as something said or done to excite laughter or amusement—a thing or person laughed at rather than taken seriously. Don't misunderstand, I wouldn't give a Funk *or* Wagnall for all the jokes in the world if you don't learn how to use them right. To paraphrase the bard's bit, "the joke's the thing," but only if it's in the right hams. Maybe Bill knew what he was doing when he put the "Ham" in Hamlet.

The everyday, garden-variety, amateur comic could be anybody. Except for occasionally modeling their ladyfriends' chapeaux or convulsing someone who missed his footing with "Enjoy your trip. See you next fall," they have nothing that sets them apart in a crowd. They don't necessarily have funny faces or funny shapes—they don't even have funny bones. On a busy, foggy intersection an ordinary human could brush shoulders with one of These Persons and never even know it. They've infiltrated high places in politics, in finance, and are found even in the restricted country clubs. I mean, some of your best friends could have joke files where their hearts should be and only a cardiogram or too many vodkas might ever bring it out.

I hope to show you how to make funny in one easy book,

13

or at least start you on the road to being a red-hot riot. It might be a little bumpy with a lot of steep hills to climb, but you can make it if you want to. You can be a comic!

Many "civilian" friends (those that aren't in show business) have made it through my joke books, thereby gaining me a lot of rivals and losing me a lot of things wholesale! Many of these pals have sprung from the ranks of the healthy, normal citizen and been converted into successful, neurotic, rank comedians. There are humans in every walk of life who run to their gag file at the drop of a joke. Myron Cohen used to be a silk salesman on the road. Now look at his "route": The Copa, Latin Quarter, Las Vegas, etc. Or take a gander at Sam Levenson, the Brooklyn schoolteacher, whose class today numbers in the millions. Could be this book will fire up other raw talent and show them the art of Do-It-Yourself comedy.

Now, leave us take f'rinstance the case of Irving. Irving, to quote his own modest words, is a highly famous comedian. He's on your radio station once a day, on your TV channel four times a month and on his analyst's couch five times a week. He's like any other nice, normal, crazy mixed-up kid of fifty-three.

Irving was born of ordinary parents. His mama was a bearded lady and so was his papa. He was the only child of three brothers and sisters. He was a shy, retiring lad; the only kid who ever retired at sixteen without ever having worked. His mama coddled him because she saw something in him that nobody else saw. She saw that he was nuts. Whilst other kiddies were cutting out paper dolls Irving was cutting up real, live comedians.

When he was twelve years old and in the 7th grade, his favorite pastime was marbles. A bully began copping a couple from him every day, and when he'd lost all his marbles, he decided to go into show business. He figured anything's better than working. He scraped together all the money he could rob and bought a *Joey Adams Joke Book*. Then he bought another. And another. And another. And when he had eight, he traded them in for one *Joe Miller* book.

When he was fourteen years old in the 7th grade, the teacher caught this poor but dishonest boy stealing answers off another kid's test paper . . . a definite symptom of humorosis borrowiasis—otherwise known as joke-lifting. When the principal begged him to explain, he said, "Well, a funny thing happened to me on the way to the cloakroom . . ."

Years passed but he didn't. Here he was seventeen years old and he'd moved to the 6th grade. When he married the principal his mama suggested he quit school to earn enough money to keep him in joke books. Then he had a baby, which upset him because it was he who had it not his wife. However, when the doctor commented that the baby had a better delivery than he did, he decided to forget his theatrical aspirations and invade the business world. He became a carpenter. One day he nailed together some nuts and bolts and screws and they all fell apart. "Goodly gracious," his mama shouted, "the boy's got a screw loose" so back he went into show business.

His family complained he wasn't bringing any bread into the house. Corn, yes, but bread—no! But did that bother a staunch, fearless, talented, great show-must-go-on trouper like Irving? Yes! However, he laughed at them (which was the only laughs he ever got) and grabbed a little joke book and a lotta friends and began comeding. Nothing happened. Then he collared an audience of his daddy's employees who'd laugh him up if he recited his Income Tax Return. And he did. And they did.

Immediately he made up what little mind he had left and, upon hearing his mama say to his papa, "That Irving's a big joke," he announced, "Daddy dear and Mummy dear, I are going to be a comedian." "Better you should be a bum or something steady like a dope peddler," cried the family.

Irving wanted very badly to be a successful M.C. He tried and tried but he couldn't make it. Finally he divorced his old hag wife, grabbed himself a sexy chorine and—y'know what? HE MADE IT! But he found that it didn't help his career any.

Somebody suggested he go to school so he could understand what the audiences were talking about when they weren't listening to him. For years he went to school at night, though he never learned anything because that particular school closed at 3 P.M. It was while he was going to school that he first got his break. The surgeon placed his arm in a plaster and in a few months he was as bad as new.

Poor Irving. He burrowed his pointed scalp deeper into his joke books until he began telling funny stories even in the morning. Got so he couldn't crawl out of bed until he'd done three minutes of material. He actually began punning when he was alone. He was no longer a social-joker. Eventually, in serious condition, he enrolled in G.A.—Gagsters Anonymous. They told him not to think about ever making jests again, but just to promise himself that he wouldn't tell them for that day. They told him if he ever woke up at three in the morning with an uncontrollable urge to throw a punch line, he should call a certain number and they'd send Milton Berle over to sit with him until the spell was gone. One night after doing this he fell into a stupor, talked in his sleep, and Berle wrote all his routines down and did his act in Miami.

Irving became a has-been who never was. He became a neurotic. He did odd things like tell other comics they were good and he said kind words about his confreres. When this occurred, well-meaning friends took him away.

'Tis said all comedians are neurotic because they have insecurity complexes. This is a lie. I know many clowns who are completely secure—and are neurotic. However, I do resent people saying we are abnormal, poorly adjusted individuals who require psychiatry. And I am not alone in my resentment. My psychiatrist feels the same way. . . .

Irving eventually recovered from this experience because he had faith that someday someone would recognize him. Several months later when he was walking down the street with his yo-yo, his kindergarten teacher stopped him and said, "Say, aren't you Irving?" and knowing he'd been recognized gave him confidence and he grew and grew. When he'd started in show business he was only five foot three inches but soon his ego was six foot two.

Today, dear, sweet, stupid Irving has gone the way of all

other successes. He has a Cadillac with a built-in Rolls. He is at home in country houses, winter houses and a coupla houses that aren't exactly homes. He is a sports enthusiast and plays all games. Friends say he even likes the outdoor athletics. He makes a grand ten grand a week. His hunting lodge in the Virgin Islands is so big he has to take a taxi to the bathroom. His faucets pour only champagne—domestic, of course, since he's always been chintzy with a buck. He has solid-gold silverware, diamond inlays and takes weekly "humble lessons."

But, you ask, is he happy? Would he do it all over again? Was it all worth it? Do I think comedians can laff happily ever after?—Yes, he would, it was, and I do. . . .

Like Irving, let's assume that all Americans think they are born joke tellers and poker players. Salesmen were the first joke carriers with their smoking-room stories, as they traveled from coast to coast selling their wares and above all, themselves. Instead of a "hello" they would greet you with "Have you heard this one?" In those days without radio or television a funny didn't get around so fast. Today, a comedian tells a new joke on TV; the next day it's old and the next week the comedian's already a has-been.

The most important thing is to sell yourself as well as the joke and do the type lines that fit. Decide what kind of funnyman you want to be. Are you a wit or a humorist? A joke teller, satirist or clown? These are the basic types, but there are other categories, such as Fred Allen's description of Ed Sullivan as a "pointer": "He doesn't do anything except point to the actor to go into his act." Arthur Godfrey calls himself a "personality" who gets a few laughs now and then. There is still another species we would come up with if we were to cross an Arthur Godfrey with a Fred Allen. The result would be Steve Allen, a personality with a wit.

The parlor or table comic who wears his wife's hat for a snicker will find himself in enemy territory when he tries to "murder the people" in the outside world. Sometimes your kinfolk snort at an old wheeze to be polite. Don't judge its reaction by their reaction. Tell Mommy a sexy joke and she may throw you out of the house, but the same fireball at a stag may bring down the house. Beware of this "friendly enemy" and make sure the gem you tell suits your listeners like Liz does Eddie. For instance, say your brother-in-law's an accountant (most of them are) so try this one: "You can't win when you make out your income tax. If you're wrong, you go to jail, and if you're right, you go to the poorhouse."

Comedy is no laughing matter to the professional comedian. A meeting of these minds, preparing for a comedy show, looks like a wake in full bloom. Making funny is a fine art that requires the right paint and the right brushes. Take the proper mixture of instructions, blend with practice and experience, and go out and create a picture of a comedian. But remember the immortal words of Will Shakespeare: "If at first you don't succeed—get outta the business so there's more room for us . . . !"

PART I

CHAPTER 1

THE WIT

AND THE HUMORIST

IF you're the type gent who gets bugged at certain things in life, like when the headwaiter digs just you and your ladyfriend standing all alone, with nobody around, not even a busboy, and mutters "How many?" do you get the urge to purr, "Seventy-eight, please." Or if you're the kind of character who crouches in a movie theatre and when a friend approaches and asks, "Hey, what are you doing here?" you answer, "Brushing my teeth, what do ya think?" Or if you're the kinda gal who, when asked "May I have this dance?" replies, "Sure, I don't want it." Or-r-r, when the switchboard operator singsongs, "May I ask who is calling?" jabs back with, "No! You may not."

Well, buster, if you got a kick like this you have the makings of a football player, a wit or humorist.

The wit thinks while he's talking or, even worse, while you're talking. He transforms experience into humor. A wit doesn't tell "jokes"—just spins a humorous web of life and expression. But in this web he catches someone or something and it's at their expense he "makes funny." And believe me, a wit's bite is far worse than a black widow's. He has to have people around him—he's like a bandleader whose band didn't show up—what's he gonna do with the baton?

At the next party you drop into or are thrown out of, try to spot this sinister fellow. There are varying degrees of wits.

The first guy who shows up at our little masquerade party is very sensitive and defensive and comes dressed as a porcupine. The instant someone gets too close and rubs him wrong, he shoots out one of his sharp needles. This might be called needling a person and *he* might be called a lot of other things. Type Two dresses as a gangster, enters with shotgun akimbo, levels it at his opponents and lets them have both barrels, spraying the room with his verbal pellets; but before he can reload, he usually gets loaded. Then there's the dry wit. But one nip of booze and he's as all wet as the rest of us. Generally the wit convulses everyone, except his grim-faced victim and a small lynch mob that waits for this party to leave the party.

On the other hand, which is in my pocket, the humorist doesn't care much if he doesn't get big laughs. (Just big money.) He will settle for a smile or a chuckle or even a pat on the head, depending on what's in your fist when you're patting him. He is not as aggressive as the wit who's more interested in the brief hard-hitting home run. The humorist makes use of longer comments thrown out for the listener to savor, whereas the wit usually dishes up something too hot for the listener to stomach. Another difference: the humorist comes prepared with categories of jokes whereas the wit relies on quick thinking to capitalize on the immediate situation. You might be able to spot the humorist as the guy who leaves the room to think of remarks he can ad-lib later. Then again, he might just be going to the john. Or both.

For a closeup of the gulf between the wit and humorist, leave us look at our great mirth men. Humorist Herb Shriner comments about his Indiana home town: "Well, usually it's pretty slow weekdays but on Saturday night we go down and watch 'em give haircuts." Another Shrinerism: "Of course I've been to Europe. I was there during the war; you know about World War II, don't you? It was in all the papers." Compare these amusing comments with the devastating scalpel of Fred Allen when he was speaking of Jack Benny: "Jack is the only fiddler who makes you feel the strings would sound better back in the cat." Or take the great humorist Robert

Benchley when he gave one of his "lectures" on falling me-
teors. "It's going to be a tough season for people who bruise
easily"; or Tennessee Ernie Ford's remark: "I'm as nervous as
a tomcat in a roomful of rocking chairs." Both remarks were
not really aimed at anyone in particular, but get a load of this
angry Allenism about network executives: "If the United
States can get along with one Vice-President, I don't know
why NBC needs twenty-six."

Wit, along with humor, must be topical either in a general
sense, such as today when we lampoon Alaska, rockets to the
moon, Governor Rockefeller, etc., or it must be timed to
the immediate situation, such as a woman who's guzzled a
little too much might evoke the witticism, "She's a lush
blonde turned blonde lush."

Will Rogers was the master at roping in the situation.
Following his confinement after an appendectomy, he said,
"People couldn't have been nicer to me if I had died." Will's
first funny crack was during a Wild West show at Tony
Pastor's: "Spinnin' a rope is fun—if your neck ain't in it."
He had a friendly feud with all film writers. His regular
greeting to any scenario scribbler: "Hi, boy, what you spoilin'
now?" Of course politics was his prime target. Rogers drily
dropped the classic "YEP—the U.S. never lost a war or won a
conference." One of his best was, "We are a nation that runs
in spite of and not on account of our government." He loved
to rip Congress. "I might have gone to West Point," he announced, "but I was too proud to speak to a congressman."

"Anybody can be a Republican when the market is up,"
he drawled, "but when stocks is selling for no more than
they're worth, I'll tell you, being a Republican is a sacrifice."

When someone called attention to his ungrammatical use
of the word "ain't" he answered, "Maybe 'ain't' ain't so correct, but I notice that a lot of folks who ain't using 'ain't,'
ain't eatin'!"

"Grammar and I get along," bragged Will, "like a Russian
and a bathtub."

Will was considered a healthy wit, but now we come to

what some call the "sick wit." He spares nobody including himself. Oscar Levant cracked, "They asked me to be on *This Is Your Life,* but they couldn't find one friend." About Eddie Fisher and Liz Taylor he snarled, "How high can you stoop?" When Zsa Zsa's name was brought up he sneered, "She does social work among the rich." Levant even had a typical Oscar for the sweet Dinah Shore. "I can't watch her," he said, "I have diabetes." Levant explains himself by saying, "I'm like Eisenhower, once I make up my mind I'm full of indecision." Henry (acid wouldn't melt in his mouth) Morgan explains Oscar Levant away by saying, "People who watch Oscar are like people who stand on street corners waiting for an accident to happen."

Groucho Marx also lets his quips fall where they hurt. He dropped by to see Abel Green, the famous editor of *Variety,* who was out. So Groucho left his marksmanship. *Was in to see you—glad I missed you.* He even used himself as a target. When asked to join the Friar's Club, he answered, "I wouldn't belong to any organization that would have me for a member." One of Groucho's best demonstrates that the shorter the remark, the longer the pain. He was sitting in a hotel lobby when an attractive woman approached and asked him, "Are you Harpo Marx?" Groucho replied, "No, are you?"

Henry Morgan is one of the bright wits and humorists of our time, in the tradition of the late Fred Allen. Henry once lost a sponsor for announcing on his radio show, "Life Savers are gypping the public by drilling the middle out of the centers. If they would give me all those middles, I could start my own company and call it Morgan's Mint-Middles." The listeners laughed. The sponsor, however, didn't think it was so funny. But that didn't stop our boy, who continues to kill his listening audience and the sponsors in one swell foop. Morgan's weather forecasts have become famous. "High winds, followed by high skirts, followed by me."—"Weather muggy, followed by Tuggy, Weggy and Thurgy."—"Tomorrow snow, followed by little boys with sleds."

Many comedians have a great wit but are not considered

in the same class as Fred Allen or Will Rogers. (What teacher could handle Allen, Rogers, etc., in the same class?) Most of these comedians use only half a wit (I had to shove that in somewhere) and the other half-prepared jokes, but their effect is no less devastating than that of Allen or Rogers.

CHAPTER 2

THE MURDERERS

THESE killer wits—the murderers—have completely overtaken our comedy field. Of course, there's never been any such animal as a sweet comic. Comedy is not funny if tender or rare. It must be well done to be effective.

Our murderers don't get the chair unless it's the center one on some dais to trigger the slaughter of a poor, unsuspecting guest. This honored guest must withstand the twenty lashes of jokes, no matter how deep they cut. And the gag can be mightier than the sword! Remember, laugh and the world laughs with you. Cry and you're a poor sport!

Comedy must be at somebody's expense—even your own. Comics like hatchet man Jack E. Leonard have left longer-lasting scars than Zorro.

In this era of masochistic comedy our most famous personalities have accepted testimonials, just to be carved to pieces by our modern murderers. The Friars, Saints and Sinners and dozens of other organizations pride themselves on the massacre of the honored guests.

Stone-faced Ed Sullivan guffawed his ulcers out when the funny men took him apart on his own TV show with millions viewing the autopsy. Jack E. Leonard stabbed, "There's nothing wrong with you that reincarnation won't cure." Phil Silvers jabbed, "You don't have a wrinkle in your face, you shouldn't either—you never move your face." Jack E. hatcheted, "Everybody says Ed has a dull personality. That's not true. He has no personality at all." Morey Amsterdam'd, "They keep sending Sullivan to Europe to find new talent but the trouble is they keep sending him back." Jack Carter added, "He takes big stars and makes unknowns out of them." Morey said, "Ed knows a lot. He just can't think of it." A New York *Daily News* editor edited, "He hasn't an enemy in the world but all his friends hate him."

Milton Berle received a razzamonial given by the Television Academy and even Uncle Miltie got bombarded.

Tom Poston said Berle started a trend in TV—a trend of comedians being canceled.

"But he *did* start comedy on TV ten years ago," persisted a Berle booster.

"Yes," agreed Tom, "and this year he finished it."

Steve Allen injected, "Milton is the only triple-threat man in the music business. He writes the song, he sings the song— and he buys the only copy. Milton would be the only composer," Steve added, "that would live to be unknown."

Arnold Stang, Milton's comedy cohort in his early TV shows, said that Milton "knows the secret of making people laugh," and concluded, "He sure knows how to keep a secret."

Even Tallulah Bankhead got into the razzing. She was asked if she had ever found anything in common with Milton Berle. "Yes, we used to get our dresses from the same dressmaker."

Jack E. Leonard, born with a silver scalpel in his mouth, spares nobody, not even himself. Jack claims his homicidal barbs are a defense mechanism. "I was so fat, I couldn't fight and I couldn't run, so I used my brain and my tongue." Jack salves his bleeding targets by announcing that he only needles people he likes.

Julius LaRosa approached Jack's wife one day and asked if the fat one was angry at him. "Why do you say that?" asked Kay. "I dunno," Julius frowned. "He just passed and didn't insult me." About Joe E. Lewis Jack said, "No matter how drunk he gets—he keeps drinking. Lewis is the only man I know that has an honorary liquor license." He said to Frank

Sinatra, "You're an Italian exclamation point." To Frankie Laine: "You have a nice voice, one of these days it will reach up to your throat."

When he's invited to "honor" a friend, the gags and blood flow freely—even if it's his. About himself he says, "I'm not exactly bald. I simply have an exceptionally wide part." Fat Jack, who will never headline *The Thin Man* series, lost a ton of weight but still eats more for breakfast than Sinatra weighs. He admits Sinatra is The Voice, Durante, the Nose. As for himself . . . "I'm Leonard the Lump!" And he adds, "You heard of the Streetcar Named Desire? I'm the Freight Car Named Leonard." Jack E. will leave no gag unturned.

To CARMINE DE SAPIO: "He's the Italian Boss Tweed."

About ERROL FLYNN: "He's here, courtesy of the Simmons Mattress Company."

About HARRY HERSHFIELD: "He's so old he refereed the Lincoln-Douglas debates. He even took Bernard Baruch to school."

To dour-faced GEORGE S. KAUFMAN: "And a happy Halloween to you, too."

About GENE AUTRY: "He's so rich he owns a Cadillac horse."

About COMO: "I always enjoyed your voice, even when you worked under the name of Crosby."

About NBC president GENERAL SARNOFF: "If he ever got mad, he could turn off the whole world."

To a bad BOSTON AUDIENCE: "If I was Paul Revere, I'd never have warned you."

To STEVE ALLEN, when he appeared on Steve's TV'er: "I could stand up here and be very funny but I don't wanna change the format of this show."

BERLE to JACK E.: "If you had three chairs you could have your own panel show."

JACK E. to BERLE: "If you had four jokes you could have your own comedy show."

JOEY BISHOP about JACK: "He's on the critical list at Slenderella."

JACK E. to GLEASON: "Go back to your dressing room and lie down on your cots."

Another killer on the wit parade is a newcomer called Don Rickles. He loves to bleed the hams that feed him. The stars pay big tabs wherever he is operating just to get cut up. To Groucho Marx: "When you lose the duck the show goes off the air." To Dean Martin: "You're not relaxed on-stage, you're boozed up." To Jerry Lewis: "A comic maybe, a singer —forget it." To Jane Wyman: "I saw you in *Johnny Belinda* and I thought your lines were great." To Milton Berle: "Are you in show business, sir?" To Harry James: "Your lip is gone, why don't you hum?" To Sinatra: "I saw you in *The Pride and the Passion* and the cannon was great." To Esther Williams: "Grease up your body and swim around the room." To Zsa Zsa Gabor: "There's a bus leaving for Budapest."

One of the wild wits of a few years ago was a lovable character called Jack Zero:

"I've had my reading glasses changed six times," he admitted, "and I still can't read. It wasn't until my last change that the doctor discovered the reason—I'm illiterate." Jack was given a plaque commemorating his thirty-five years in show business. "That's very nice," he said, "now if you'll find me a room I'll have some place to hang it." Zero's favorite target was agents. Some time ago an agent died and a collection was taken up for funeral expenses. Jack was asked to give $5 to the fund. "Ya want $5 to bury an agent? Here's $10, bury two agents."

Even in the highest places, our gag men have infiltrated where politicians fear to tread. According to the Murderers, Ike was asked, during the Adams-Goldfine scandal, what he was going to do about the Civil Rights Bill. "I don't know what to do," the President responded. "I thought Goldfine paid it."

Even the politicos' kiddies are on the hate parade. The sons and daughters of Democrats like this one—"I don't care what you're President of, get your golf balls off my lawn."

Henny Youngman has mellowed with age. But, like any fine bottle of old champagne, he explodes if you tip him the wrong way. I wouldn't want to be around when he blows his cork. "Where you from?" Henny asked a would-be heckler. "Brooklyn," was the reply. "Well," said Henny, "there's a bus leaving, get under it." To one group of annoyers, he ripped, "Don't move! I want to forget you just the way you are." To another he knifed, "Some people bring happiness wherever they go; you bring it whenever you go." To a pest, "There's a pair of shoes with three heels on them." Henny loves to make his wife a Youngman accident victim. "My wife," he croons, "has a slight impediment in her speech. Every once in a while she stops to breathe. My wife," he says, "has her hair cut in a pet shop. Her hair color is changed so often she has a convertible top. And when she goes to bed she packs so much mud on her face, I say 'Goodnight, Swamp.' " Henny says he stayed in one hotel where the room was so small the mice were hunchbacked. "I had a room and bath," he bragged, "but they were on separate floors."

Alan King was speaking at a dinner in England when VP Nixon showed up. "Dick is here," quipped Alan, "to register Ike in the British Open Golf Tournament."

Max Asnas, sage of the Stage Delicatessen, when he heard a rival restaurant burned down: "I'm sorry to hear it but it's the first time the food's been hot in his place."

Of course, these lines, like dynamite, are dangerous in the hands of unskilled personnel. A Murderer must be prepared to take the consequences. So, like the sign says: DANGER—PROCEED AT YOUR OWN RISK.

CHAPTER 3

THE ANGRY YOUNG MEN

THERE is another class of working wit that is busy murdering people on a different level. A new uprising in the comedy world are the Angry Young Men. Some of them are angry old men, but the one thing they have in common is that they are all steamed. Like any volcano that's ready to burst, they gotta open their mouths to let the hot air out.

These angry comics don't bother with the American humorist's surface irritations, like women drivers, parking, mothers-in-law, or nagging wives. These sick sick comics have been packing the night spots with customers who come to read their fever charts in public. They find humor in such taboos as religion, politics, homosexuality, dope addiction and matricide.

This satire stuff isn't exactly new. Men like Henry Morgan were picking on the world before some of our angry young comics were in it. Many current brooders claim that the present crop of perturbed, social-critic funnymen trace hunks of their material and attitudes back to the old Henry Morgan diatribes against society in the early days of radio.

Henry agrees, in part. "But there are many differences," he yawns. "Mainly, whatever I did in social criticism stemmed from a well-fed, usually employed young man who wasn't against society—just bemused by it. The new boys actually seem to be mad about something, but in addition, it's a lot more calculated. They get a set of comments together, re-hearse them for twenty minutes in little saloons, then pray for a shot on the Ed Sullivan Show. If they get it, they're hailed as the new comic voice of the New School of Satire. *Time* magazine devotes columns to their wit and intelligence. They wear sweat shirts while they work to show that they defy society and its materialistic soul, but drive home in Jaguars to show Mamma that they were right—they shouldn't have become dentists in the first place."

As they tell me in Danny's Hideaway: "It takes one to know one."

The sound and fuming of Mort Sahl has been reaching into the highest places. His mental processes have been de-fined as "irreverent with an extra dose of social satire and without benefit of censorship or hypocrisy"—whatever that means!

"Humility," he says, "is the worst form of ego. It's usually indulged in by people who can afford it— He's a wonderful guy, so humble, this millionaire." Here are some typical com-ments made by this comic critic as he gets angrier and angrier with every step . . . on the way to the bank:

> I saw a folk singer at the Waldorf working in a skin-tight velvet shirt open to the navel—and he didn't have one; which is either a show-business gimmick or the ultimate rejection of Mother.
>
> I am against analysis, along with the Church and the Communist Party, because it turns you against your folks. On the other hand, I always enjoy Arthur Miller because before the second act is over, I get a chance to hit my father. The best thing about analysis is that if you don't make it with 'em, they'll refer you to another analyst. They call it rehabilitation-referral-motivation therapy. We call it fee-splitting.
>
> Mothers love to suffer. No matter how successful their sons are, they say, "Let me do your wash as long as you are here. Please, let me take it down to the coast and beat it against the rocks."

Right in the middle of the Lebanon Revolution, Ike went to Gettysburg for the weekend. Lots of people thought he was out of touch, but I understand he took a radio with him. The actual headlines here said, MR. KHRUSHCHEV THREATENS AMERICA. RED CHINA WARNS BRITAIN; but down at the bottom of the page, in small print, was the headline—OIL COMPANIES UNEASY.

Los Angeles now has thirty-one Bohemian spas selling cappuccino and espresso in which you can meet women who are defiant Bohemians, who have broken up with their families for the evening, wear no make-up and do not concede to combing their hair. Gad, what nonconformity! They usually smoke a lot; smoking is almost always a sign of defiance with women, defiance of convention, and they usually smoke mentholated filter-tip cigarettes through a holder, which I guess is okay, if you can't become a nun.

The newest comic proponent of social significance is a young man called Lenny Bruce, who is ready to fight the world at the drop of a gag. He is proud to be called "The Rebel with a Caustic Cause." Mrs. Bruce's bad little boy answers the showers of critical hailstones that have assailed him: "I'll always be accused of bad taste, especially by people who eat in restaurants that reserve the right to refuse service to anyone."

When his name was mentioned to Ed Sullivan for a TV appearance, Ed asked what safeguards he would have against the use of questionable material. Bruce suggested electrodes taped to his heart. "If I say anything wrong—*zip*—I'm dead. It could be a TV first!"

Nobody escapes Lenny's brain whip, from the President of the United States to his fellow performers. He murders an American comic who, having forced his agent to book him into the Palladium in London, lays such a big egg that he is reduced to urging his English audience to bomb Ireland.

At a mine disaster he has a promoter growl at a child, "Get away from there, kid, stop kicking dirt in the hole."

The trial of a G.I. for shooting a Japanese woman brings

this bulletin from a Tokyo commentator: "So sorry. Verdict has been changed from life in prison to two weeks at Waldorf Astoria."

Lenny admits he isn't going to change the world. "But certain areas of society bug me, man, and satirizing them, aside from being lucrative, provides a release for me."

"By any moralistic yardstick," lectures our sick sick hero, "Jimmy Walker was certainly a more heinous figure than some poor schlub I read about that breaks into a warehouse and steals a couple of tires. So, the public raises its eyebrows at this handcuffed, unshaven villain and Hollywood eulogizes Walker by making a picture of his life. It's the old cliché— there's no such thing as a little pregnant." Lenny admits, "We're all hustlers—we're all as honest as we can afford to be."

Another member of the new school of angry young men is a very literate comedian called Shelley Berman, who says he is angry at nobody—it just turns out that way. Shelley doesn't want to change the world—oh, maybe a few things and people here and there. But mostly his act is "an enormous confession, a very personal account of my own foibles with the assumption that the audience has experienced like misadventures, or at least can understand or empathize."

Like his fellow members of the "Jack the Ripper" Club, Shelley likes to amuse by abusing the things that bug him. Only it's a little tough to stay angry when your belly is full and so is your bank account. Shelley picks on everything from buttermilk to flying. "I think," says our hero, "if airline travel is properly defined in Webster's dictionary, it should read, 'hours of boredom interrupted by moments of stark terror.' "

The "Un-Angry Man" spouts:

> Airlines are always bragging about their safety records: "Flying is the safest way to fly. Statistics prove that flying is the safest way to travel." I don't know how much consideration they have given to walking.
>
> Propaganda efforts on the part of the commercial airlines are terribly confusing. I haven't the slightest doubts about my safety in a plane, until I walk into an airport terminal

and realize there is a thriving industry in this building selling Life Insurance policies—GOOD FOR ONE FLIGHT—which is very cautious. They have booths selling them—even slot machines. I may be confident about landing safely but there is a serious note in somebody's mind that I can make it.

Shelley claims that his group is much more literate than the "inside" comics. "We do not use the joke, per se (no punch line at all). Our deliveries are radically different from the general style of comedians, which has existed for so long." Berman picks on people like André Gide.

> He was a Frenchman, and that makes him a little dirty to begin with. We remember him very well because, first of all, he was never Premier of that country, and secondly, he won the Nobel prize for literature of that country. Now, the thing that Mr. Gide wrote about mostly was, unfortunately —forgive me—homosexuality.
>
> Well, he liked it. He thought the world should live that way and he spent his lifetime recommending it.
>
> Well, anyway, he got the award. Which makes me a little doubtful about the judges.

Here are some Bermannerisms:

> I don't like buttermilk—it's not the buttermilk that bothers me—it's the way the glass looks when you're through that makes me sick.
>
> *Reader's Digest* occasionally comes out with those shock articles like "The Truth about Girl Scout Cookies" by Bertrand Russell with footnotes by Havelock Ellis.
>
> A University of Chicago student is this: If you give him a glass of water he says, "This is a glass of water, and if it is a glass of water, why is it a glass of water?"—and eventually he dies of thirst. When he comes home and his mother says, "How are you, son?" he says, "Relative to what?" And what the hell can you say after that?

Sometimes Shelley makes odd statements like: "Remember the trouble Louis Pasteur had selling rabies? Nobody wanted

it." Or: "I can't figure out why Erskine Caldwell is seeking
success. He can have so much fun just sitting around and
thinking."

Another one of the Angry Young Men is an old-comer
called Phil Leeds. He is only angry because he has been picking on the world before some of these angry come-latelys
learned how to pick their teeth. He says:

> It's easy to get work nowadays if you work cleaner, better
> and CHEAPER, than anybody else.
>
> I come from a neighborhood where the only sound you
> hear is an occasional call for help. When I was a kid, my
> living room was decorated as a swamp.
>
> I started in show business by working in a small trio— It
> was so small there were only two of us.

Phil's stories are way out. Like the one about the eight-
year-old boy who came home from school and put on a dress,
lipstick, make-up and high-heeled shoes. When his mother
caught him, she screamed, "If I told you once I told you a
thousand times—don't play with Daddy's things."

Phil likes to talk about his early girlfriends. "I met her,"
he muses, "while washing my hands in the subway. Her phone
number was on the wall—she was well recommended."

The popular charter member of the angry ones holds his
meetings in New York at the No. 1 Fifth Avenue Bar, where,
like his happy fellow crusaders, he picks a subject and lets
go. His sermon for today is GREETING CARDS:

"They have all kinds of new cards now like 'Happy Thursday,' 'Congratulations on your new sink,' 'Many Happy Returns to Macy's,' 'Good Luck on your 25th and Last Payment
on your Frigidaire.' "

Phil likes to read some of his favorite cards:

> Get well, lazy bones, get well get well
> Get out into the Woodland dell
> The birds are chirping in the sun
> And you are missing all the fun
> Of Mother Nature's carousel

There's nothing wrong with you
So get along with you
I can tell, I can tell, I can tell
So get up and get out
Of that silly little coffin
And get well, get well, get well.

Here's his special:

I heard they took your insides out
And left you good as new
You'll soon be up and round about
The same old dear old you
Of one thing I have no doubt
How nice it could have been
If once they took your insides out
And stuffed your outsides in.

Another one of the "way out" boys is Ronny Graham. He was sour on society before it was sweet to do it. As one of the original angry young men, Ronny was dropping barbs on the "squares" way before it became the famous national pastime. Graham likes to aim his sights at the behavior pattern of America's middle class.

Professor Graham's favorite lecture platform is "The Downstairs at the Upstairs," where his class of beatniks and hipsters worships at his shrine. They come to cheer his marksmanship as he slings his intellectually guided missiles at the world around him.

Ronny suggested a new dance called

DOING THE PSYCHO-NEURO-TIC:

You dream while you're dancing.
And if you dance with Henry Luce's wife
That means that you're in love with *Time* and *Life*.

My little boy could have his choice of girls every night
But my little boy says nay.
Yes, my little boy is crazy, he's not right
Or could it be he's gay?

Graham's fables won't replace Aesop but they have found their own audience.

> This is the strange story of a strange child named Sphere. He was called Sphere because he was a mistake all around. When he was six years old, his parents suspected he was a monster. Instead of pulling wings off flies, he would pull them off houses and small institutions.
>
> By the time he was five—he was eight.
>
> He was seven feet tall and weighed 300 pounds with his fountain pen empty.
>
> His parents became alarmed and called in the famous child psychologist, Doctor Sigmund Schmuckler of Vienna. Doctor Schmuckler was a very talented man and if he had gone to school two more years, he might have become a chiropodist. He was famous for his theory that children should be obscene and not curbed.
>
> The doc asked the kid, What do you want to be when you grow up, and the kid answered, An orphan.
>
> And in two days he made it—the hard way.

The professor keeps his students apprised of all the news: "I just read that a young boy of nine played chess against fifteen of the world's greatest experts, all at one time, and would you believe it—he lost every damn game."

Although Ronny is of the abstract school of comics, he doesn't hesitate to curb the abstract school of painters. One "smearist" artist asked him what he thought he should get for a big canvas he had just completed. "Six months," said Ronny.

Graham comes up with a Shaggy Dali Story: It concerns a thief who breaks into the artist's home and remains there long enough for Dali to study him and give detectives a sketch identifying the criminal. Within 10 hours, thanks to Dali's sketch, police arrested 22 poodles, 9 giraffes, 2 corkscrews, a wire recorder and a talking horse named Foxhunter who refused to talk until he saw his lawyer!

The humor of Jonathan Winters is far out of this world. Like one of his play characters—"Man, I don't dig society and

they don't dig me"—Jonathan is "bugged" by almost everything and everybody and is ready and willing to take on all
comers.

Once on the Jack Paar Show he introduced Zsa Zsa Gabor
as "one of the famous Gabors." This didn't please Zig Zag,
who felt she is THE famous Gabor and immediately took him
to task. "Oh, well," sighed Winters, "you *are* an elderly
woman." And once when some pretty fresh young thing
called him "Fatty," he fumed, "I'll be the same when I'm
twice as old watching the crows walk around your face."

I wouldn't say Winters is an angry young man—he's furious!
He describes Madison Avenue as the place where "they took
the padding out of the shoulders and put it on the expense
account."

If Jonathan is attacked, it brings out his heavy artillery.
One heckler at ringside caught a 21-gun salute that our boy
aimed right at him. "I've got just the thing for you, friend.
A do-it-yourself Ox-Bow incident."

When Ed Murrow visited the Winters family on *Person-to-
Person,* Jonathan was warned by his friends to "behave." He
promised but it was tough for this offbeat comic with the
macabre sense of humor who *hates* the expected and con-
ventional. "Good evening, Ed," he greeted Murrow. "I am
Jonathan Winters. This is my wife. These are my children.
This is my living room. I'd like to show you more of my
house—but there isn't any more."

Personally, I don't think any of these Angry Young Men
are the least bit angry—or even peeved. It's tough to be
annoyed with a loaf of gold under each arm.

If these way-out comics keep marching on the "In" comics
and taking shows away from them—the only Angry Young
Man will be *ME!*

CHAPTER 4

JOKE TELLER, CLOWN
AND SATIRIST

ANOTHER form of comedian is the joke teller, who specializes in retailing humor that he bought wholesale. A good technician must have timing, confidence, delivery, and the right joke in the right place. Timing is a feel that comes with experience at throwing the punch line. Confidence comes after your first snicker. The more laughs you get, the stronger your delivery. If you don't believe in yourself and use your own personality, nobody else will.

The right joke in the right place depends a little on your brain file of gags or your gag file of brains. Pick out the gems you like, tell them over and over in your style, and then file them away in your funny bone for future use. If you want to make funny, you must become a joke collector. Remember, if you steal one gag, that's plagiarism; if you steal a lot of gags, that's research. Milton Berle became famous as a professor of research.

Don't misunderstand, I ain't encouraging you to steal. As an amateur, you gather jokes that you feel suit but when you're in the big leagues you must hire a gag writer to keep fresh and new. Many great storytellers are great technicians—but couldn't create a belch after a Hungarian dinner.

Instead of firing your ammunition on somebody else, make yourself the butt. Jack Benny created his own cheapskate role. Jack admits he has a pay phone on his wall at home. "When

I see a check in a restaurant," he says, "I get a slight impediment of the reach." Benny once paid me the highest compliment on-stage at the Chez Paree in Chicago. "I like your show so much," he gooed, "I'm going to pick up my own tab."

Any comic that's open for business has a storeful of mother-in-law, wife and kid jokes. It's always funnier when it's told about his family instead of somebody else's. The great dialectician Myron Cohen quotes his own mother, who never quite captured the English language or its idioms but tried to keep up with the modern jargon. She heard her children use the expression "out of this world." One day whilst enthusing over something she had cooked for her family, she exclaimed, "This soup is out of town!"

Jesting about your own wife is always funnier than putting it on some other poor soul. "My wife gave me a choice of a new fur coat or a nervous breakdown." Or, "All my wife knows about good cooking is which restaurants serve it." It's always more amusing when you make yourself the patsy.

Humility has become an important word in show business ever since Godfrey fired Julius LaRosa, thereby making him a millionaire. Knocking yourself down makes the audience sympathize with you. When I returned to my television show after an absence of a few weeks, I announced, "There was a big sign to greet me when I entered the studio. It said WELCOME HAM—JOEY ADAMS." Another time, when I signed off my radio show, I said, "Well, it's time to say good-by for another week. My cast, my crew and I are leaving, you know—my studio audience left twenty-five minutes ago." Here are some more wrecking bits on myself:

> This program comes to you live from New York—at least it starts out live—it sometimes dies in twenty minutes.
> There has been talk of putting our radio show on film, if they can find anyone with nerve enough to develop it.
> I am what is known as a low-pressure comedian. But I'll straighten that out as soon as they find the leak.

Alan King, the comic, has proven quite successful in England. He was tapped for a command performance. Just before going on he peered through the curtain at Queen Elizabeth and her relatives. "I kept thinking about my background, my environment, and this had me a little scared," he said, "but the thought that almost put me in a panic was the realization that these people once even looked down on an educated man like George Washington."

The long-winded joke teller, or storyteller, follows a slightly different set of rules. Myron Cohen, George Jessel, Lou Holtz and Sam Levenson are all masters of the long story or anecdote. With these guys it's not so much the success of the punch lines, but the build-up that keeps them healthy and working. It's the way they tell the joke that counts, and from what I can tell, it's the money that counts.

The storytellers are masters of vivid description, perfect dialect, detailed character sketches, and present a joke as clear as a technicolor cinemascope movie. Sometimes their stories are even longer. The storyteller has always relied heavily on dialect as his strongest technique, but recently his stock in trade has been threatened.

Censorship plays an important part in comedy on television. The mildest joke is deleted if some VP figures it will offend one child on a farm someplace in Omaha. The gag doesn't have to be blue, but you won't get the green light if the non-censor only thinks that somebody will see red when they hear the line. Fred Allen once described one of these vice-presidents as "a person who finds a molehill on his desk in the morning and must make a mountain of it by 5 P.M." Only Bob Hope, who is known as the sacred cow of joke tellers, gets away with almost any type of line. In talking about Bishop Sheen, Ski-nose said, "The Bishop is making a western—the title is going to be 'Sheriff of Vatican City.'" When the Bishop was opposite Milton Berle on TV and started to beat the funnyman's rating, Hope cracked, "Well natch, the Bishop has a better writer than Berle."

Censorship has practically eliminated the dialectician. This has become a very sensitive age. Only a few laugh years ago, a dialectician was an honorable profession. It ranked number one among storytellers. Today, because of the Hitlers and

Nassers, the fights in Little Rock, the threats in the Middle East and the fear of communism, everybody has become supersensitive and ready to fight at the drop of a gag. Do a Jewish dialect story and the Anti-Defamation League is down on you. Reference to a Negro sics the N.A.A.C.P. after you. The Irish, Italians and Germans have their own American societies waiting and ready to challenge anybody who makes with the jokes about their people. This is a very serious era for comedians. You never know when the wrong story will touch off the laugh powder that will explode in your face.

Of course, in the hands of a real pro, dialect is still a fine art. Only experts like Myron Cohen have survived. Dialect King Cohen likes to tell about the two partners in the cloak and suit business who were having an argument. The senior partner said, "You're so crooked that the wool you're pulling over my eyes is 50 per cent cotton." Or the one about the two Jewish women in Brooklyn who were talking and one said to the other, "If I live, I'll see you Wednesday—if not, Thursday." The late and great Bill Robinson, the foremost Negro star of his time, used to get howls with the one about a little colored soldier who tried to break out of camp and was stopped by the guard. Our hero challenged the guard with, "I've got a mother in heaven, a father in hell and a girl in Harlem—and I'm gonna see *one* of 'em tonight!"

You can't picture an Irishman as a drunk or an Italian as a rough guy or even a Scotsman as being tight, no matter how funny the joke is. One Irish comedian said on radio the other day, "In the part of Dublin I come from it's no disgrace to get drunk—it's an achievement." Next day thousands of letters came into the station from members of the Irish Society demanding an apology.

I have appeared at dozens of benefits for Boys Town of Italy and Italian-American organizations all over the country. But when I cracked in a newspaper interview, "When I was in Rome I saw a very unusual Italian movie—*the heroine was flat-chested,*" I was severely reprimanded by some Italian pals.

You are much safer ribbing your friends, especially if they are there to take it. Such as, "Jack and I have been friends for ten years. For ten years there's nothing I wouldn't do for him and there's nothing he wouldn't do for me, and that's how it's been for ten years—we don't do a damn thing for each other." Again, it's the right joke at the right time. If you're at a dinner to honor a pal, anything will be accepted, no matter how hard you hit, as long as it's high enough.

Fred Allen re Garry Moore: "Garry will one day be the oldest boy on TV."

Jack Benny, asked to speak for a buddy, said, "When George thinks, it's a violation of the Child Labor Law." In speaking at a dinner for a famous glamour girl, Earl Wilson said, "She is one of the ten bust women in America and is number one on the Community Chest." He referred to Jane Russell as the "treasure chest" and added, "I saw Jane in a low-cut bathing suit that revealed her two best features."

At a banker's convention, Will Rogers ribbed the whole gathering. "Gentlemen," he said, "you are as fine a group of men as ever foreclosed a mortgage on a widow. I'm glad to be with you Shylocks."

One of the rare forms of comedy storytelling is double talk. This is often used for commercial purposes by politicians and lawmakers without due credit to the master of this art— Al Kelly. Doing "double" is like reading an eye chart. Al once said to a head doctor, "I can't qualm my prite on account of my coltique." After listening to him for fifteen minutes the psychiatrist threw away his couch and when last seen was running for Congress.

Al Kelly and I went to Lindy's for a midnight snack. The waiter asked Al for his order. "I'll have some ungahockte luckinmember with tsidreckte aringemixt—easy on the sauce." The waiter, slightly confused, figured he'd come back to him after he got my order. "What will you have?" he asked me. "I'll have the same," I said.

The three most common forms of double talk are:

1. FADE-AWAY DOUBLE. The voice of the speaker keeps getting softer and softer until your ears are practically in his mouth. You think you have A.C. ears and he has a D.C. voice.

2. FRACTURED ENGLISH. The right words put in the wrong

places. Speaker sounds like he's breaking in a new set of teeth.

3. DROWNED ENGLISH. The speaker says nothing—but with expression. You feel that he should gargle with crushed razor blades.

When you begin to understand these guys, you are really in trouble!

The clown, even with his mouth closed, can overwhelm an audience with his antics. He sees life as though it were reflected in a fun-house mirror, with all its weird and exaggerated effects. A clown will take things out of life and distort them, twist them, blow them up or mold them in any way to achieve his goal. Charlie Chaplin reversed a real-life situation when he once sat down next to an elderly woman. He glanced at her and she immediately gave him a very contemptuous look, whereupon Chaplin slapped *her*. There was nothing too sacred back in the days of Chaplin and W. C. Fields, when they would reverse life situations by kicking dogs, children and old ladies. Today a comedian would never attempt this before an audience. Most of them wait until they get home to do these things.

Another technique of the clown was to start with a small incident and build it until it approached catastrophic proportions. Laurel and Hardy were famous for this. In one of their pictures they were caught in a traffic jam on the highway, with cars lined up bumper to bumper. Laurel and Hardy accidentally bumped the car ahead of them, which touched off a chain reaction resulting in complete chaos: People fighting, ripping off fenders, breaking windows, throwing fruit, smashing cars, until the entire scene looked like an auto junk yard. These guys were capable of starting a world war by merely stopping to tie their shoes.

W. C. Fields used a similar building technique in his famous golf game, where for eighteen minutes he prepared to strike the ball . . . and never did get around to hitting it. Fields may have missed the ball, but was always proud of the fact he hit the bottle.

Chaplin employed a still different type of build in his role as a waiter. In going from the kitchen to the customer's table Chaplin had to cross a large dance floor with a roast duck. As Chaplin stepped out onto the dance floor the orchestra struck up and the floor suddenly became crowded with people, engulfing Chaplin, so that all we could see was the tray of roast duck held high in the air, bouncing all over the floor. Some college letter men show up and eventually the whole thing turns into a football game, with Chaplin carrying the roast duck tucked neatly under his arm.

You might have noticed that in all of these examples each clown created a certain amount of tension, leaving the audience in an anxious state of mind. That is, would Chaplin ever reach his customer with the roast duck? Or would W. C. ever hit the golf ball? This tension, through the antics of the comic, is relieved and the result is laughter. ('Tis been burbled by some critics that I have often relieved tension just by leaving a stage.)

When the clown goes into his act, he invariably uses a prop, whether it be a hat or a bobby pin. Very often a clown will speak little or no dialogue, so the prop aids him in conveying thoughts, ideas, etc. Chaplin used his cane ably as part of his character, showing that he is a little man who needs "a cane to lean on." However, he also would find broader uses, like poking people with it, hooking it on a railing, tripping someone with it, etc. A clown will find a million and one uses for his prop, depending on his character and his immediate surroundings.

Another characteristic of the clown is that he will go to any extreme to "make funny." Jerry Lewis has walked into a swimming pool with all his clothes on just for a laugh. In the movie *Casablanca*, Harpo Marx was leaning against a building when Groucho came up and asked him if he was holding it up. Harpo smiled, walked away and the entire building collapsed. Charlie Chaplin in one of his films was on the job at a shipyard when the foreman told him to find a small piece of wood. Chaplin looked all over but couldn't find one, until he spotted the piece he was looking for under some pilings. Chaplin proceeded to pry loose the piece of wood. He finally yanked it out from beneath the pilings and then to his horror looked up and discovered he had launched a huge ship, as it went sailing down the launching platform.

From Emmett Kelly to Olson and Johnson to Red Skelton we've roared from the first bust in the mouth to the last pratfall. If we were to take a situation, for example just setting a door on the stage and putting to work all our great clowns, here's what might happen.

Charlie Chaplin would approach the door and before he could open it, a large fat lady would come through from the other side. She would become wedged in the threshold, as Chaplin stood watching her struggle to get through the narrow opening of the doorway. He would attempt to help by trying to pry her loose with his cane and soon become entangled with her, pinned between her and doorway. Unable to move and almost suffocating, he'd then try to push her out, but find a tough time locating a spot at which he could apply pressure.

Abbott would open the door in Costello's face and then Costello, holding his nose, would proceed to walk right into the wall next to the door.

A closed door for Olson and Johnson is a simple feat. They would merely have three midgets, two giants and a two-headed monster take a battering ram and knock the door down.

Laurel would go to open the door, but Hardy would stop him, insisting that he go through first. Hardy would then open the door first, only to have a bucket of water fall on *his* head.

Red Skelton, in his drunken stupor, would stagger up to the door and start pulling frantically on the knob. He'd pull and pull until a sweet little old lady would appear. Skelton would tip his hat as she opened the door *inward,* to Red's dismay.

Jacques Tati, the great French clown, would walk up to the door, begin to turn the knob, only to have it come off in his hand.

So next time you go to open a door, be careful, you never know who's going to be on the other side.

Like the song says, "Be a clown, be a clown, be a clown . . ."

You'll notice much of what the clown does is satire. Red Skelton at the tag of his TV show would be saying nighty-night to the audience when suddenly he would be yanked from sight by having two guys grab his ankles from underneath the curtain and pull back. In addition to its being a surprise, what we laughed at was the complete loss of dignity that resulted. Red, with his falls into orchestra pits, slipping on banana peels and his tripping over shoelaces, is the best loser of dignity in the world.

Chaplin also used this "loss of dignity technique" as a true satirist. Seeing life from the underside, as a tramp, gave him opportunity to poke fun at life. One of his great films, *Modern Times,* lambasted mechanization and industrialization, complete with speeded-up production line, a time-saving device to feed employees while they worked, and a large television camera whereby the president could watch everyone at all times and naturally catches Charlie in the washroom, resting. Or in the same picture, after his nervous breakdown on the production line, Chaplin is advised by a doctor to take it easy and rest up. All Charlie does is to walk out into the street, and is engulfed, with people rushing past, cars speeding by, horns blowing, babies crying, children yelling, and his point is easily made.

Perhaps the only comic to come close to Chaplin is TV's eight-year wonder, Sid Caesar. If there is any word to describe his technique, it's exaggeration. From his intimate vignettes on the adventures of a fly ("Look at that crazy moth, every night instead of going to bed he's throwing himself against that light bulb, knocking his brains out") or the thoughts of a three-month-old baby ("Ugh, here comes Aunt Sadie with her wet kisses") to the broad satires of movies, operas or television shows, Caesar's a true master of satire. His exaggeration technique may be seen more obviously in his sketch of a woman putting on make-up, when she begins to put on the lipstick. Instead of merely keeping to the outline of the lips she is soon tracing the imaginary line of the lipstick up to her ears and around her eyes and down to her reputation.

Related to Caesar, not by blood but by money, are radio's Ted Brown and The Redhead and Bob and Ray. Bob and Ray's radio shows and brief TV stint kept many giggling through the commercials they never had. It's no wonder, since they satirized almost every commercial on the air. 'Tis rumored they got together with Henry Morgan and wrote a book called *Sponsors We Have Lost*. They used many of Caesar's techniques, but Bob and Ray were more verbal. Where Sid would go through detail visually, they would do it verbally. Their satires included everything from Senate hearings to soap operas. Some of their soap opera satires were "Mary Backstage, Noble Wife," which asked the question, "Could a girl from a small mining town out West find love and happiness in a small mining town out East?" or, "The Lives and Loves of Linda Lovely." Their famous interview satires started a whole new trend. One interview concerned a man who trained dogs to run on a baseball field during the game, another was about a man who reconditioned worn-out shoelaces for a reasonable price.

A few years ago when all the cigarette companies were singing, "I can do anything milder than you," Bob and Ray started a series of classic interviews, which went something like this:

RAY: Good evening. Tonight we're going to interview one of the crack news commentators, Preston Sturdly.
We then see Preston (Bob) sitting on top of a large pile of newspapers.
RAY: Preston, I understand you're always on top of the news.
BOB: Why, yes, I am.
RAY: Can you tell me why you like being on top of the news?
BOB: Sure, I like to read newspapers and keep up on current events. I like newspapers because they tell the news, they're easy to read, the print is large and above all, they're milder, Ray, much milder.

*End of interview and also of any prospective cigarette
sponsors.*

Stan Freberg trots closely on the trail of Bob and Ray with
his satires on *Dragnet,* the Army-McCarthy Hearings and
many popular songs. His underplaying parallels Bob and
Ray's, but often on record he becomes as broad as Caesar.
He was probably one of the first to poke *Dragnet,* with "My
name is Thursday, I don't work on Fridays." Freberg also cut
a record on the Calypso songs, where his singer–bongo-player
got so loud that Stan had him backing away from the mike
until he was in another room. In saloons he tosses wacky
opening lines like, "Well, I've just secured the musical rights
to *The Bad Seed.*" Considered a nut by many, Freberg lives
in a nice quiet padded room—padded with money.

Another top satirist is Ernie Kovacs. One of his more
famous bits is his jest of the Coty Girl commercial, where we
see the top of the Coty Girl's hat and as she slowly tilts her
head upward, as in the original commercial, she looks straight
at the camera and smiles, only to get a pie in her face. On a
television show a number of years ago Kovacs would literally
tear up studios to achieve his goal. (Sometimes I think his
goal was just to tear up studios.) Often, to end his show
differently from other TV shows, he would have the studio
"blown up" by having falling bricks, fire, smoke, a screaming cast and quick sign-off. One of his funnier lampoons was
on *The Hit Parade.* One segment of it concerned a pretty
girl sauntering up to the camera, and when she smiled we
saw the number "3" written on her front teeth. She then
stuck out her tongue, which had the name of the number 3
song written on it. Whenever Ernie does a TV show he always
gags up the credits at the end of his program:

Lighting by Electricity.

Costumes by Clothing.

*Associate Producer Robert Jones, the only one who would
associate with our producer.*

Directed by Harvey Smith.

Harvey Smith directed by Mrs. Smith.

In a way, Kovacs has the visual scope of Caesar and the verbal dexterity of Bob and Ray.

Under the heading of satire, we must also include parody, irony and travesty, which go hand in hand, like Tinker to Evers to Chance. Parody is a satire of song, such as Joe E. Lewis' parody of "The Anniversary Waltz." "Oh how we danced on the night we were wed, we danced and we danced, 'cause the room had no bed."

Irony pertains to the routine's unexpected outcome. Menasha Skulnik jokes about the college professors who give a million dollars to a great philosopher to find out what life is. Finally after a year passes, a friend asks the professors if they found out what life is and one of the professors replies, "What do you mean, we haven't even found the philosopher." Another example is the one about the young chick who is having trouble getting married. Finally in desperation, her mother suggests she put an ad in the paper. The girl puts an ad in the paper that reads, "attractive, young homemaker desires companionship of man seeking same." After a few days the mother asks her daughter if anyone answered her ad. The daughter hesitantly replies, "Yes—Daddy."

Travesty refers to a satiric treatment of a serious work, such as a treatment of the Gettysburg address, the Constitution, or as seen in this next example, Shakespeare. There was a group in Chicago a few years ago known as the Compass Players. This little-known group included the now big knowns, Shelly Berman, and Mike Nichols and Elaine May. They set Shakespeare's *Hamlet* in a delicatessen, as if it had been written by Paddy Chayefsky. Hamlet stood dramatically behind the counter with a side of corned beef in his hand and said, "To cut or not to cut."

Satire is used by all comedians, but the ones I've pinpointed use it more extensively. Steve Allen and Co. have done a satirical sketch about adult westerns, Jack Benny spoofed *Gaslight*. Then there's Buddy Hackett and his famous Chinese waiter monologue. Guys like Caesar, Bob and Ray, etc., have made satire their place in comedy.

CHAPTER 5

IT TAKES ONE TO
KNOW ONE

SO what's your niche in comedyland? The categories I've mentioned overlap one another. That is, Red Skelton is an A number one clown, but he still makes with the monologues and many of his monologues have a satiric base. So there is really no rigid line separating the different types of funnymen—except income brackets. A comic will excel in one phase and still utilize all the other techniques as part of his over-all "personality." So don't pick your style off a pipe rack. Be custom-made. Select the material that fits you. Don't pattern Bob Hope when you're a natural clown without using words. Picking what suits you is something that shouldn't be done overnight, unless you're in Alaska where the nights are six months long. Take your time, watch as many comics as you can and steal from the guys who steal from the best.

If you were to take a bunch of the different types of comics and shove them all into one room, you'd probably go nuts . . . which would give you a head start in becoming a comedian.

Recently, the March of Dimes voted me "The Man of the Year" and gave a testimonial dinner in my honor at the Waldorf-Astoria Hotel. All of show business showed up and the target for the evening was me.

My friends were ecstatic. Jan Murray screamed, "Man of the year? What year? Who voted? I demand a recount!"

Morey Amsterdamned, "It's fitting we give Joey Adams a dinner—everybody does—he hasn't picked up a check in twenty-five years—but that's on account of his religion—he's a devout cheapskate!" Harry Hershfield was eloquent in his praise: "After listening to twenty-two speakers, all I can say is, anybody needing that many character witnesses shouldn't be honored."

Even the wires were barbed. Henny Youngman's telegram read: REGARDS TO A WONDERFUL GUY—ME.

Gypsy Rose Lee had often joined Earl Wilson and me in our tour of the night clubs and restaurants begging for money for the March of Dimes. She wore a low-cut blouse and asked the men to stuff their contributions in her bodice. She allowed them, even, to take change if the contribution was large enough. We missed Gyp at my dinner but she remembered to send a wire: I'M SUFFERING WITH AN OCCUPA-TIONAL DISEASE—A COLD IN THE HEAD—RIGHT WHERE I NEVER EXPECTED IT.

Earl Wilson said, in his opening remarks as toastmaster, "Broadway has the strange custom of publicly razzing some-body it likes and tonight's victim is Joey Adams." If they liked me any more, they would have honored me right out of the business altogether.

Morey Amsterdam kicked it off with, "Joey knows a lot—he just can't think of it. The trouble with Adams is that he was born with a handicap—his mouth. Don't misunderstand, Joey is my friend, I like him—I have no taste—but I like him."

Jack Carter, an old friend, naturally swatted me with some new lines. "The things he does for his friends," Jack said with his arms around me, "can be counted on his little finger." Jack got sentimental, "This dinner for Joey has me all choked up—with jealousy. . . . Joey," he continued, "works for every charity committee. The other day he joined an organization so small, they didn't give them a disease yet.

"When Joey started in the business," Carter remembered, "he worked at Leon and Eddie's. That is now a Kinney Park-ing Lot. Then he worked at La Martinique which is now a cellar. After that he worked at Loew's State, which hasn't had vaudeville since—and right now, he's working on the Waldorf-Astoria."

Jane Kean was a pal way back when I wrote my first book. As she told it, "Joey had a switch on the etchings bit. When he wrote *Gags to Riches,* he asked me to his home to read the proofs. In the first place, I've handled literary wolves before, and secondly, my mother is very strict—so I took him to my room instead."

Red Buttons heaped his praise on my philanthropic work. "Fooling around with charities," was the way he put it, "has made Joey a very rich man." Red reminisced, very affectionately, that I gave him his start in show business by giving him a job in the Catskill Mountains, better known as the "Borscht Belt," at $1.50 a week. "From this huge salary that tightfisted Adams paid me," he recalled, "I sent my mom 50 cents, I gave my brother 25 cents, and the rest I gambled away like a dope. . . . Very few people know," Red said warmly, "that Joey was an inspiration for Castro. He figured if Joey fought his way out of the mountains . . ." Red admitted I was the originator of the fountain pen that wrote with sweet cream. This was used in the summer resort where we worked. Because the places were all "kosher" the dietary laws forbade dairy with meat and I hated black coffee, so I filled my pen with cream and wrote into my coffee. Red claims I made a fortune on the side by selling it to the guests at a quarter a squirt.

When Buttons noticed Sessue Hayakawa in the audience, he raved about the great Japanese star. "The time I beat out Mr. Hayakawa for the Academy Award," Red reminisced, "Sessue was very gracious—we both bowed, and as I bowed, I got knifed."

The former five-times world's boxing champ, Tony Canzoneri, reminded everyone of the day he joined my act at the Steinway Theatre in Astoria. He showed up two minutes before curtain and I was furious—as furious as I could get with a five-times world's champion. "We go on in a minute," I perspired, "aren't you nervous?" Tony's answer was simple: "I fought Barney Ross in the Garden and 20,000 fans were there to see me defend the lightweight title, friends bet millions on me, Barney could knock your head off with a right or a left, I received $100,000 for the fight and I wasn't the least bit nervous. Here I'm getting about four dollars a show, there are eleven people in the audience and nobody can hurt me—so what the hell do you want me to be nervous about?"

Horace McMahon talked about my childhood. "We tried to dig up somebody who knew Joey when he was young—and we'd probably have to," he said. "Everybody knows the late and great Fiorello, Mayor of New York, raised Joey, but what they don't know is that LaGuardia was a parole officer at the time."

Harry Hershfield related the saga of when I was dating a beautiful young lady whose father objected. "No actor will ever be a son of mine," he warned. "After seeing Joey act," Harry explained, "the father told the girl not to worry—she could marry him—he's no actor."

Everything reminds Harry of a story. He told about "the actor who was cremated and had 10 per cent of his ashes thrown in his agent's face."

Myron Cohen brought me some of his pet new jokes as an outright gift. "I might as well give them to you and make an honest man of you," he grinned, "you'll only steal them anyway." Myron's favorite concerns the little Italian man who walked into the bank looking for the man in charge of arranging loans. The teller said to him, "I'm sorry, sir, but the loan arranger is not around." "Okay," he said, "then I'll talk to Tonto."

Cindy's favorite was the story of the happy couple celebrating their silver wedding anniversary at their sumptuous home on Long Island. Everybody was happy; that is, everybody except the husband. He was glum. When his lawyer came in to congratulate him on his 25th anniversary, the husband screamed, "You louse! You bum! Remember when I was married only five years to that dirty dog and I asked you what would happen if I stick a knife in her and you said I would get twenty years in jail? Well, tonight I would have been a free man!"

The audience's favorite was about the drunk who accidently stumbled down the subway stairs and reeled up another entrance still loaded. "Where ya been?" asked his friend who was waiting on the street. "In the basement of a friend's house," hicc'd the drunk, "and boy, has he got a set of trains!"

Earl then introduced Lou Holtz. "I never played the mountains like some of the stars on this dais," was Lou's opener. "I was born a star." Then he caressed my shoulder and crooned sweetly, "I'm glad to be here tonight because there's only one Joey Adams—I found that out by looking in the telephone directory." He continued affectionately. "This boy has a lot of talent—but it's all in Al Kelly's name."

Naturally, Lou couldn't leave without one Lapidus story . . . sixty-seven-year-old Sam Lapidus was getting complaints from his wife about their romantic life. "I am not the man I used to be," apologized Sam. "I ain't got it—I had it—but I ain't got it." A friend tipped Sam to visit a Dr. Slotsky for "hormonies." "Are they good?" Sam asked. "Good?" hollered his friend. "When a horse got to go to stud they send him first to Slotsky. If he can fix up horses imagine what he can do for you." Four weeks later, Sam Lapidus met his friend who inquired, "Well, did you see Slotsky?" "Every day for four weeks," Sam beamed. "Did it help you with your wife?" his friend wanted to know. "Wife nothing," answered Sam, "but yesterday I ran a mile in 1:48."

Jack E. Leonard took care of me in very short order. "Joey," he sliced, "has a great sense of humor. He doesn't care whose it is." Then he finished me with, "This kid has a great delivery. He should be with Western Union."

Hermione Gingold was the next star called on to *honor* me. "I'm delighted to go to a dinner for Joey Adams," she started. "In fact, I'm delighted to go to any dinner on Sunday night—it's my maid's night off and I'm a lousy cook." Hermione recalled she got to know me when we were appearing weekly on a panel show with Henry Morgan, Morey

Amsterdam and Dagmar. "It was my first show on radio here and who do you think gave me good jokes, who do you think got me a cup of tea when I needed it, who do you think encouraged me?" she asked. "Henry Morgan! ! !" Miss Gingold, wishing to introduce a note of culture to the proceedings, said she'd asked Tennessee Williams to write her a speech. The following is the pure, unadulterated Tennessee Williams speech as delivered by Hermione in her veddy, veddy Britttttish accent: "I first met Joey at Jack's place—he took my hand and talked to me like the rain. 'Big Mama,' he said. I said, 'Ha.' And Joey said, 'Don't give me that crap.' Then Joey put on his oxygen mask and I liked him better that way. . . ."

Henry Morgan was the next killer. "My only regret," snarled the acid one, "is that we all together missed *Maverick* tonight." Henry recalled that "Joey and I were on this show called *Sez Who* for two years until CBS found out what we were doing there. Anyway," announced Henry, "I don't know what I'm doing here—I'm pretty unique—nobody even invited me to this thing."

The next executioner was Steve Allen who opened with "Maybe nobody invited Henry Morgan but I'm even more unique—Henry invited me!" Steve, who came right from his TV show, apologized for not wearing a tuxedo or even a dark business suit. "It's been such a long time since I did any dark business. . . . I've been asked to talk about Joey's books," he continued, "and I recommend them highly—and if I weren't, I couldn't." When Jack E. Leonard, who appeared on Steve's program that night, guffawed loudly, Steve said, "You were very funny up here tonight." "I thought so," admitted Jack. "Too bad you weren't on my TV show," cracked Allen. Steve segued right back to my literary career. "Joey always felt he could write. One day, in one of those cheap magazines, he spied an ad that said, 'How do you know you can't write?' Seeing that ad fired Joey to send in his jokes, anecdotes and other masterpieces. One month later he received a telegram which said, NOW YOU KNOW YOU CAN'T WRITE."

Up came quizmaster Jack Barry. (Jack Leonard had announced that Barry was going to lecture on "Honesty.") "I have been asked to speak about Joey Adams' success on television. Well, good night," said Barry, sitting down instantly. George DeWitt was even shorter but just as devastating. "I'd love to say something nice about my friend Joey Adams, but I just can't think of it."

Jan Murray swept on furious. "I don't understand this whole bit," he fumed. "Who the hell elected him Man Of The Year? We started together. I'm better looking than him. I have a daily TV show. He's made Man Of The Year and I can't even get chosen Jew Of The Block! Don't you think it's a little incongruous?" By now he was screaming. "They toss this little jerk a big dinner at the Waldorf—and Bernard Baruch is sitting on a park bench by himself! Don't you think it's blasphemous when Joey gets a gold plaque and Albert Schweitzer's trophy room is empty? Don't you people notice anything wrong? Here Joey is being honored by the March of Dimes and Dr. Jonas Salk can't get an interview on a local radio show."

As I went down for the last time, Jan's finish—and mine, too—was the truism about my appearance, many years ago, at the now defunct La Martinique saloon in New York. It was my first big time night-club job and I followed Danny Kaye, a tremendous hit, and Danny Thomas who'd been doing capacity business for eight consecutive months. I opened to twelve people; the second night business fell off a little. Dario, who owned the room, was preparing to hang himself. The third night there wasn't one person in the joint. I stopped Dario, just as he was about to shove his head in the oven. "I can't understand what happened to my following," I mumbled just for want of something to say. "Your following?" he bellowed. "Your following? What did you do to mine? ?"

Smith and Dale, who have starred in show business for over 60 years, stated that I was the one who started them in the business. They said, "Joey received his first award from the President of the United States and it was a very proud moment because Abraham Lincoln very seldom gave out those kind of things."

Al Kelly was touchingly sentimental in his praise of me. "My pal Joey and I have stuck together through thick and thin," he said huskily. "Joey got thick and I got thin." Al went on: "When I first started with Joey I was very poor— but then I got used to it."

I knew my dear wife, Cindy, would save me—and she did— for the knockout. "We've been wed for seven years and I think married life is wonderful," she began; "it's just Joey I can't stand. I don't know why they say Joey is cheap," she added. "He gave me ten dollars off on my ticket tonight . . . and, besides, there are lots of other wives who chip in half on rent." Cindy blew me a kiss, then continued, "Of course, many people thought our marriage wouldn't last because my husband is so much older than I. I don't think he's so old, although recently he did receive a brochure from an old age home—and it was marked *Urgent*.

"So what if my Joey does have little eccentricities? F'rinstance, he doesn't wear glasses and he can't see. He thinks I don't notice it but the other day he walked into a closet and barked 'Down!' And I did get a little nervous when he met me in the lobby and said, 'Good evening, sir.' "

Chairman Earl Wilson introduced his co-chairmen in the newspaper world who had made the event possible and, in fact, who'd made me possible. Great guys like Lee Mortimer of the New York *Daily Mirror,* Hy Gardner, New York *Herald Tribune,* Louis Sobol, New York *Journal-American,* Frank Farrell, *World Telegram & Sun,* Danton Walker, New York *Daily News,* Nick Kenny, New York *Daily Mirror.* These great Fourth Estaters wrote my name in their papers when I couldn't afford to list it in the telephone directory.

Other great stars like Dolores Wilson and Robert Merrill of the Met "sang my praises," Johnny Ray "cried" for me, Jayne and Audrey Meadows prettied up the proceedings and Richard Kollmar, who recorded the evening for his next A.M.'s Dorothy & Dick Show, graced our dais. Dozen of fiddles from Chez Vito serenaded me to ease my wounds as Sessue Hayakawa, Christine Jorgensen, Lanny Ross, Jack Pearl, Sammy Kaye, Congressman Si Halpern, Attorney-General

Louis Lefkowitz, Carmine DeSapio, and many other judges, politicos and celebrities of assorted shapes, sizes and salaries laughed their approval.

Of course all of our town's night club and restaurant fraternity, who have done so much for the March of Dimes, showed up and paid $100 to eat food they could get free in their own joints. Thanks to my pals Vito Pisa of Chez Vito, Ed Wynn of the Harwyn, Gene Leone of Leone, Dalmo Pozzi of Danny's Hideaway, Sal Cucinotta of Teddy's, Max Loew of the Viennese Lantern, Jack Silverman of the International, Max Asnas of the Stage Delicatessen, Duke Zeibert of Duke Zeibert's in Washington, D.C.

Mrs. LaGuardia, who with the late Mayor of New York, Fiorello H. LaGuardia, helped raised me, beamed her approval. "Fiorello would have been very proud," she said. "Our Joey . . . he's a good boy."

Mayor Wagner then summed it all up. "I'd like to thank all the people of the entertainment world who have done so much for every charitable cause. He who stoops to help stands erect before his fellow men."

We managed to seat 600. We turned away 100 more. And to show the real spirit beneath the gags and ribs, I was able to hand over more than $25,000 to Frank Berend and Ernest Frost on behalf of the theatrical division of the March of Dimes.

PART 2

CHAPTER 1

THE ABC OF COMEDY

WHICH is more important, the material or the delivery? That question has been plaguing comedians since Joe Miller. It's like asking: which came first, the chicken or the egg? And brother, if you don't have the right chicken, you can lay the biggest egg, no matter how good the delivery.

Laughs make the world go 'round, especially if you have a good round of jokes. Anybody can be a comedian, anybody can tell a joke, but you must learn your trade and sell yourself as well as the joke. In order to tell it well you must learn it properly. Nobody can learn to paint in one day. You can't become an expert dancer in one lesson no matter what Arthur Murray guarantees. To tell a joke correctly you must repeat it over and over again to everybody you meet. Tell it with confidence and, most of all, use your own wording.

The punishment must fit the crime. There is no such thing as an old joke—if it fits it's new. For instance, a speaker on the dais following a long line of gabby talkers will get a lot of results with the opening remark: "I was a young fellow when these speeches started" or "I will be very brief because I know that the mind cannot accept what the seat cannot endure."

And never give yourself away. Don't preface with "Here's a joke," or let anyone introduce you as "one of the funniest guys in the world." After that, it's like trying to follow a world

59

war with a pop gun. I remember at a Friar's Club meeting, Adlai Stevenson was a guest speaker, but he had to follow Fred Allen. Fred was in rare form that night. Finally when Allen finished, amidst thunderous applause, Stevenson weakly rose to his feet. "Gentlemen," he said, "before the meeting I was out in the lobby talking to Mr. Allen and he confessed to me that he didn't have a speech for tonight's occasion. I graciously gave him my speech. So you have just heard it." And he sat down instantly. Go top that.

Another thing, steer clear of cliché-ridden intros like: "And now without further ado . . ." Or, "And now here is a person who needs no introduction." (Usually this character needs it more than anyone.) Or, "Here is a great guy you all know." (He forgot the poor soul's name.) Or, "I've had the pleasure of working with this next performer many times . . ." (In the post office during the Christmas rush.) You can easily louse up a whole act with a stale introduction. Of course, you can also louse up a good introduction with a crummy act.

Suppose you were addressing a Chamber of Commerce meeting where the discussion of the day was traffic. You could wallop more across with a good laugh, if it is appropriate, than any dramatic presentation. A good opening line could be "Three out of every four automobiles in the world are in the United States and two of them will get to the parking space before you do." Now that's telling a story for the need for parking facilities and you segue from there. Remember, you didn't telegraph that this was a joke. Or you might use a line like, "The only way to get to the other side of Main Street is to be born there." If you wish to suggest traffic cops be nicer you might quote, as an example, "The California police are so polite that when a lady driver sticks out her hand to make a turn, they kiss it."

If you throw the right jokes you can even make the losers laugh in Las Vegas. Everybody will be on your side if you put yourself in the same boat as they are—even the sore winners. My opening line when I play a gambling room is usually "I hope the owners have more luck with my money than I did." Or, "There is only one way to beat the gambling

here—when you get off the plane walk right into the propeller." Or, "I come here every year to visit my mother, and
leave a little interest." It isn't necessary to sympathize with
the losers. Just louse yourself up and they'll forget all their
worries and laugh at you. "Nobody forces you to gamble,"
I say. "Nobody forces you to have sex either but it's more
sociable." They love it when you kid the gambling business:
"Even the parsons flip a coin—double or nothing. The justices
of the peace are the biggest gamble of all—from the picture
*When Your Hair Has Turned to Silver Put It in the Slot
Machine.*"

It isn't tough to find good lines; the most important thing
is that they fit the situation and is the kind of humor that
fits you. Any day at Hanson's Drug Store in New York, you
will find the better comics in the low-price field exchanging
five Milton Berle howlers for one Bob Hope gasser or thirty
Joey Adams jokes for one Groucho Marx job. One little
comic complained, "I can't understand it. Berle gets $20,000
a week, Hope $30,000. I do the same jokes and I don't make
enough money to pay to see these guys so that I can steal
their stuff." I actually heard two unknown comedians having
a battle royal at the table at Hanson's because one claimed,
"You better quit doing my Danny Thomas routine or I'll
start doing your Red Skelton bit."

The jokes are important only if they fit you and the situation. Sometimes it's necessary to switch a gag to make it fit the
laugh. When Bing Crosby's new wife had a new baby, every
alert comic or comedy writer used the line, "The first word
Bing's baby spoke was MONEY." This joke could be switched
to any man's rich child or you can give it the double switch:
"The dress manufacturer had a new baby boy and the first
word the kid said was RETURNS"; or "The first word clothing
man Mike Levine's son said was LININGS"; or if a comic has a
child, "The first word the kid spoke was BOFFOLA"; and so on.

This is commonly known amongst comedians and comedy
writers as "switching." Somebody used the line about the
beast of Red China when she was reminded of the tiny island
of Quemoy: "Long time no seize." Of course, this could be

switched very easily to General Nasser or even Zsa Zsa Gabor. When Zsa was working on her fourth husband, I cracked, "It's about time she got married—long time no seize." It is not tough to make the switcheroo. "Baseball is our national pastime," somebody said. "Now go and convince Errol Flynn." This could be easily switched to Trujillo, Jr., Zsa Zsa or even Tommy Manville. Flight jokes are usually very funny. Any comic worth his weight in laughs has his own flying jokes when he opens in a new town. Henny Youngman quips, "I don't fly on account of my religion—I am a devout coward." Milton Berle ad-glibs, "I just flew in from California, and my arms are tired." Jonathan Winters snickers, "I just flew in from Chicago—no plane—I had 141 pigeons Scotch-taped to my arms." It is obvious that any of these lines could be switched or played with to suit yourself. If the man is rich and plays tennis, your zingeroo might be "He has cashmere tennis balls"; or if he is a baseball nut, "He's got a mink baseball bat"; or in the case of Jerry Lee Lewis, the rich young rock and roll singer who married a thirteen-year-old child, "For a wedding present he gave his wife a set of platinum jacks"; or about some wealthy character who was squandering his money, "For a Christmas present we gave him a solid gold yo-yo."

When New York's billionaire governor, Nelson Rockefeller, beat out multimillionaire Averill Harriman for the gubernatorial race, everybody was sorry for Harriman, but Berle's writer cracked, "So what? Harriman lost New York so he bought New Jersey." When Rocky announced his new tax plans, Congressman Jim Healy gagged, "He's got plenty of loot, why doesn't he pick up the tab for the whole thing?" Even revolutions can be funny with the right switch. When Castro took over the government of Cuba, Batista, his family and his followers took the first vehicle out of town. The gags came fast and furious. One kid in school was asked, "What is the chief export in Cuba?" And the child answered unhesitatingly, "Cubans." Naturally, this could be applied to any country. Some hope this will be a Trujillo joke in the future. Even Castro's bearded men came in for their share. Henny

Youngman wired the Cuban leader: HOW ARE YOU FIXED FOR
BLADES? This is an old switch from a Monty Woolley gag or
a George Bernard Shaw line before Youngman even learned
to shave.

New Hindu Roulette: A fakir tootles his flute with six
cobras—one is deaf. Here is the switch to suit your story or
situation: The Broadway bookies are now playing a form of
Russian Roulette—six telephones are used and one of them
is tapped. The Stage Delicatessen version is: The latest game
of roulette is with bagels instead of bullets—six of them are
served, but one is without lox.

Another form of switching is done by juxtaposing one
word in a phrase or even the whole phrase. There are many
famous sayings, proverbs, oft-quoted remarks, clichés that can
be upside-downed and turned into laughter with the twist of
a word. Some f'rinstances:

I got a frog in my throat.
One frog said to another, "I got a man in my throat."

I'm so sick I couldn't eat a thing.
One cannibal said to another, "I'm so sick I couldn't eat a
person."

The kind of guy who likes to have his cake and eat it too.
The kind of guy who likes to have his cake and eat yours too.

A wolf in sheep's clothing.
I went out with a sailor—he was a wolf in ship's clothing.

A thinking man's filter.
Joe E. Lewis uses a drinking man's filter.

One alligator said to the other, "I'm gonna make me a man
bag."
One sardine to another, "Man, we're packed in here like
commuters."

CHAPTER 2

CREATING THE GAG

MAKING up a joke is serious business. Some writers are paid thousands of dollars for one line and others are paid one dollar for a thousand lines. Writers are always getting needles like this: "You mean to say you just sit around thinking up gags?" "You actually get paid for that?" "Bum, why don't you take out the garbage?" Today, with TV's great demands, no joke is really garbage. The only thing in a can is laughter. Pretend you're a high-class gag man. First, just pretend you're high class. Then choose a subject and let your mind play potsy with it, but keep it clean. Sit back, relax, close your eyes, and before you fall asleep get a vivid image of your subject— Uh-uh, I said keep it clean. If we had a mental tape recorder, here's how this stream-of-consciousness gag might shape up. . . .

Now let's see . . . automobiles, new automobiles . . . they got power brakes, power steering . . . how about "Power steering is so sensitive that even if you burp it moves"? . . . No . . . how about sneezing? Sensitive power steering and sneezing. Something like "I got a new car and it's got the most sensitive power steering in the world. I'm driving down the road and I sneezed—and whoops I'm in the other lane" . . . fair, but needs more. . . . Exaggeration is always good . . . let's see . . . maybe a sneezing attack that would make the car go toward one place, ending up in another. Yeah, maybe that's it. The final gag might go like this: "I just got a new car and it's got the most powerful steering in the world. I'm driving along and I sneeze and whoops I'm in the other lane. . . I sneeze again and I'm on the shoulder. Once while driving from New York to Chicago I got a hay fever attack and ended up in Florida."

This will give you an idea of what lines to think along. And if you don't get anywhere, well, you can always put a handkerchief in your mouth and create your own gag.

In manufacturing jokes, use images everyone knows. When it comes to modern automobiles, we think of power steering, or when someone mentions airplanes, we think of propellers, wings, etc., or when we think of golf, we think of Ike. These images that pop front 'n' center when a certain subject is the object are s.o.p. (standard operating procedure) for any joke, because they set up the punch. Without the build-up this next gag would take a nose dive.

"I was flying from New York to Chicago last week and about a half hour after take-off we hit some bad weather. The wings were shaking, I was shaking, lightning was striking, terrible thundering and the plane was being tossed around all over the place. The stewardesses even stopped smiling and all the passengers were really nervous. Finally, one of them rushed up to me and said, 'Please, do something religious.' So I did. I took up a collection."

The setup is very important. If you don't think so, try romancing a broad in a noisy cafeteria . . . just as the Four Horsemen of Notre Dame wouldn't score either if one of 'em was horsing around and didn't keep up his end. . . . Sooo-o-o, leave us not be a horse's rump!

In this next section, I lump together topics that have been rehashed often for comedy fare, such as Alaska, Sex, Russia, Sex, Hollywood, Sex. Watch closely and you'll spot the different types of creating and the techniques of building. If at the end of this book you know a pile about building and you're still not a comic, send 25c and a stamped, self-addressed envelope for my "How to Be a Successful Architect" pamphlet.

CHAPTER 3

THE MONOLOGUE

Alaska

NOBODY was happier than I when Alaska became our 49th State. Only I don't intend to go there again until it melts. I love God's frozen people but I get a chill when I open the refrigerator. Our new State is so cold even the janitors are complaining.

The first and last time I was there it was so subzero the hens laid eggs from a standing position and penguins were bringing babies instead of the stork. The only way my Cindy could part her hair was with an ax. One Eskimo advertised in the local snow-sheet that he was looking for a man with a high fever for a roommate.

Alaska is very proud of her statehood. The first day our new flag was born with a 49th star on it the stores in Anchorage were flooded with orders. One little old lady, after waiting in line for hours, finally reached the counter to purchase her flag. After looking it over she said admiringly, "It's beautiful. What other colors do you have them in?"

Since Alaska has become a State, the Eskimo population is rapidly becoming Americanized. In fact, some of them have even hacked holes atop their igloos in order to stand up when they hear "The Star-Spangled Banner."

I've been in show business all my life, but I have the most peculiar manager—he likes to book me in odd places at odd times. My brilliant representative sets me in such spots as

Boston during Holy Week, Florida in summer, Israel at Jewish holiday time and Alaska during the winter.

When I received the contract to play Anchorage, I grabbed my tux and snowshoes and off I skidded. North Pole nights are six months long. I arrived half-past January. The daytime is also six months and everybody stays up—that's why they have those arctic circles under their eyes. But I wasn't disappointed about not playing Florida that winter because I came back from Alaska with a color—blue. That country is great if you happen to be a polar bear. Oh, I was a big hit. The only trouble is the audience is a little cold. I talked to one guy for an hour before I found out he was a snowman. I had a high-class opening at the club I worked. Everybody came to the première formal, sporting tuxedos with built-in parkas and patent-leather snowshoes. The center ringside was reserved for eight—the mayor, his missus, and six huskies.

When we arrived in Glacierville, they hired a chauffeured toboggan to meet us. One of my bop musicians squealed, "Man, this country is cool." And the saloon beat is colder. After one blizzard someone opened a new café called The Snowdrift—and it was! Betty Furness began her career there as a doorman. The midnight manners in their clubs are a drag. Everybody wears white shoes and suits to match. That is, until the summer when they thaw out. A typical dinner in Alaska is frozen chicken soup, cold tamales, and iced coffee. I couldn't even buy my wife a present because my assets were frozen.

Since Alaska achieved statehood, the barbs have flown fast and furious. Alaska being bigger than Texas, the feud between these areas has made good fuel for hot comics:

A Texan and an Alaskan were arguing the merits of their respective states. No matter what the northerner claimed, the southerner insisted his state offered the same thing only better. "Just tell me one thing that Alaska has that Texas doesn't have more of?" "Well, for one thing," smiled the Alaskan sarcastically, "modesty."

An Alaskan never spanks his son when he's naughty. He

just puts him outside in a sled and turns off the electric blanket.

Many young couples are shoving off to Alaska to get married because they want to have a long honeymoon night.

"Was it cold when you were in Juneau?" a fellow was asked when he returned. "Why, it's so cold up there," came the reply, "that there are times when the sunlight freezes on the ground and then shines all night making street lights unnecessary."

If there's one thing harder than peddling a Ford to a Texan it's selling an icebox to an Alaskan.

A native from Nome, who was treated royally during a stay at his friend's home in Maine, told him, "Now I know what they mean by southern hospitality."

When I was in the Tundra those nights were so long that even some owls died of insomnia. Up there when a fellow doesn't show up for work for a few months he can always claim he took the night off.

I wouldn't say it's cold in that area where they think of Canada as the tropics but when I was there, a snowman was stationed in front of my hotel and all night long he kept knocking on the door and asking for a hot-water bottle.

The Eskimos kiss by rubbing noses. Jimmy Durante could be the Clark Gable of the Birds-Eye Country. If they don't have blankets, the Eskimos cover themselves with ice to keep warm. Four picnickers found themselves away from home with only enough ice for three—the fourth one froze to death.

A baby in Alaska swallowed its knife and fork. It would take two months before the traveling doctor would be around again. "Good heavens!" moaned the mother. "What will the baby do?" "He'll have to eat with a spoon," soothed the father.

The Martians

The Martians have invaded our comedians and comedy writers. You can't scan a newspaper column or visit a night club or watch your television without running into a Martian. They even have a song here on earth, "Take Me To

Your Leader, Cha-cha-cha." We could raise a lot of money for our planet by taxing all those Martians running around looking for their leader. Anyway, them outer space guys ain't so smart. If they had any brains they would go right to their leader instead of asking everybody for directions.

I wonder if Marsniks are telling earth stories up there. I can just picture our Martian rocketing to his home on Mars Boulevard late one night and explaining to his dear wife, "Couldn't help it, dear, I was caught in a traffic jam in New York." I wonder who's the Milton Berle of Mars? Can't you just hear him convulsing his telespace listeners about how he landed in the Bronx Zoo and told a lion, "Take me to your feeder"? "You're too late," purred the feline, "I just ate him."

Me, I know one thing: a woman will never be the first human being to set foot on the moon on accounta she won't know what to wear for the event. We are so close to it now, one guy is already manufacturing pills to relieve "space-sickness." Bob Hope has his bags packed; he has ordered his space suit and will travel. When Robert returns to earth his first joke must be about the difference in our women. "The women on Mars have their bosoms in the back—it doesn't make 'em more attractive, but it's better for dancing."

Outer space is like juvenile delinquency—the more we study it the more there seems to be. Now that our Navy is launching rockets it won't be long before sailors have a girl on every planet. Today's comedians can justifiably claim their jokes are "out of this world." I can hear you saying, "I wish they were there with them." Our Martian approached a bop musician who told him, "No use taking you to my leader—he isn't hiring tenors this week."

My favorite is the Martian who landed in New York and found he had broken one of the little wheels on his spaceship. He asked every leader in town to find him one but to no avail. That night while passing the Stage Delicatessen he noticed some bagels in the window. "I'd like to buy some of those wheels," he asked Max Asnas, who owns the joint. "Those aren't wheels," said Max. "They're bagels, you eat them." Asnas sliced a bagel in half and offered it to him. After chewing a bite the Martian beamed, "Hey, this should be good with cream cheese and lox."

One Martian ambled into Hanson's Drug Store and cornered the gaily lit-up juke box. Giving it the once-over he crooned, "What's a doll like you doing in a joint like this?"

Two gents from outer space zoomed into New York for a night on the town. Sidling up to a fire hydrant one queried, "Where is your leader?" His buddy heckled, "What are you asking him for—can't you see he's just a kid?"

An earthnik landed on Mars and noticed a big crowd around one store. Pushing his way through he spied a machine in the window. Some character pushed a button and a baby shot out. He pressed another button and another newborn babe arrived. "What kind of thing is that?" our hero asked one the Marnuts standing around. The Maron answered matter-of-factly, "That's our baby machine. Don't you make babies like that on earth?" The earthnik looked bewildered. "Are you kidding?" he said. "On earth we use a different method altogether. A couple get married, they go on a honeymoon and nine months later there is a baby." "Oh," said the spaceman, "up here that's how we make trucks."

A Martian floated into New York's Central Park Zoo and instructed one of the monkeys, "Take me to your cheetah." "Oh, I can't," answered the monkey, "he's in Africa filming a Tarzan picture."

Everybody knows that the man in the moon gets lit up almost every night so why is everybody sending him a shot?

I have it from reliable authority that there is a Communist Martian who is out to assassinate that leader the other Martians are looking for.

So this Martian came to earth, stepped into a taxi and said, "Take me to your leader." "Sorry," said the cabby, "I'm pulling into my garage."

A Martian stopped a man on the street and told him, "Take me to your leader." "Oh, I can't," answered the fellow. "She's in Florida with my mother-in-law."

A Martian landed in New York and went right to IBM headquarters. He found the machine that they used to feature on *The $64,000 Question* and said sternly, "All right. You've had your fling in show business, now you're coming home."

So this dungaree-clad Martian lands at the Actors Studio and mumbles, "Take me to your leader." "That's pretty good," a director tells him, "but come back next year—you're a little tense."

1961's Outerspace Report: The first American sputnik reached Mars and the Buck Rogers of the Martian Marines advanced toward the debarked American crew. The G.I. raised his disintegrating gun but was halted by his Commanding Officer. "But," cried our sergeant, "he looks dangerous, sir!" "No," said the officer. "Anybody with a cork stuck into the top of his neck instead of a head must be bringing good news."

A spaceship landed on Broadway and out popped a neurotic Martian who stopped a fellow and said, "Take me to your leader's psychiatrist."

When a rocket scientist got into an argument with his wife, his friends advised him to count down to zero before he lost his temper.

The Martian landed in Las Vegas and watched a series of players pumping the arm of a slot machine. The Martian stepped up to the slot machine and whispered, "I don't know what office you're running for, buddy, but try to smile a little more when you shake those hands."

The same Martian watched one player hit the jackpot. While the cherries, pears, and peaches spun around, the machine shook and sputtered and delivered an outpouring of coins. The Martian said to the slot machine sadly, "Baby, you ought to do something for that cold."

Oh, well, if you've seen one Martian—you've seen 'em all.

Texas

I'm tired of Texans bragging about the size of their state. Now it's Alaska's turn—and I'm glad . . . glad . . . glad! Just a mention of the Lone Star State and everybody from Texas stands at attention. Just hum "The Eyes of Texas Are Upon You" and any of its drunks will yell themselves sober.

Until Alaska came along I thought if I heard one more gag about you-know-where, I'd really gag. So this is the last of the Texas jokes recorded for pesterity:

There is a movement afoot to teach Texas schoolchildren how to spell the word "small."

One rich Dallas kid wanted a new playpen, so his father bought him Alcatraz. Another oilman from Houston is dickering to buy Hollywood because his kid would like to study the stars.

Trouble with those Texas millionaires is that all that money is going to their pockets. Some of those oillionaires are real cowboys—every spring they saddle up and roundup the banks. The biggest spenders aren't Texas oilmen—they are the wives of Texas oilmen. First time I saw that TV show *The Millionaire* I thought it was about the second largest state.

In Texas everything but a Caddy is considered a foreign car. On one highway between Galveston and Corpus Christi stands a sign with this legend: KEEP OUR HIGHWAYS CLEAN, NO CHEVROLETS, FORDS OR PLYMOUTHS ALLOWED.

Don't misunderstand me, I love the people of the Lone Star State. After all, Texas spelled sidewise is taxes and that's where a hefty hunk of it comes from—deep in the heart of taxes. So, what could we lose if we permit them this one last chance to howl before Alaska dwarfs them completely? Like the salesman from Anchorage, Alaska, said, "I hate to go to Texas. It gives me claustrophobia."

While touring France, a couple from San Antonio decided to send gifts to three friends from home. Sauntering into an art gallery, they picked out a Van Gogh, a Rembrandt and a Picasso. "That'll be $600,000 in American money," the dealer told them. The husband wrote out the check, handed it to the dealer and then turned to his wife. "Now that we've got the cards, let's go get the presents."

One Fort Worth resident wanted Louis Armstrong to fly his thirty-piece orchestra down to his ranch. The price was right but the king of the trumpet wanted to know how many guests would be at the party. "It ain't no party," said the Texan. "My doorbell chimes are busted and I feel neighbors who visit me like to hear music when they ring."

One six-foot-seven bruiser from Waco in a playful mood clumped over to a little guy standing at the bar (naturally, he was from out of the state) and stomped on Shorty's foot with all his might. The little man looked up with anger in his eyes and screeched, "Did you do that on purpose or is that some kind of a joke?" The giant growled, "I did it on purpose." "O.K.," said Shorty, " 'cause I don't like those kind of jokes."

Our next hero is from El Paso. He commissioned an architect to build him a house. The architect quizzed him on what kind of house he desired. "Well," drawled the Texan, "I'd sort of like something to go with my new brown suit."

Then there's the fable of the rich Texan's son (is there any other kind?) who asked Daddy for a set of golf clubs. Next day Pop called his offspring. "I got you six clubs, son," he said, "but I'm sorry one of them doesn't have a swimming pool."

A Texan was boasting that his state had never known bad times. "But surely you felt the great depression of the 1930's," someone said. "No, we didn't," replied the Texan. "However, we did enjoy one of the poorest booms we had ever known."

A 14-K Texan strode into a Cadillac showroom and told the salesman: "My wife has a touch of flu—what do you have in the way of a get-well car?"

A Texan was dictating his will to his lawyer: "To my son I leave three million dollars—and he's lucky I didn't cut him off entirely."

A Texan complained to his friend that his son seemed headed for juvenile delinquency. "I know I've neglected him," the Texan said, "and maybe that's the reason." "Buy him a present," the friend suggested. "I've thought of that," admitted the Texan, "but I don't know what to get him." "Well," his companion suggested, "why don't you buy him the Houston police department?"

One of the more poverty-struck Texans lost control of his new Cadillac and ran into fifteen other cars before he could stop. Fortunately, it all happened in his own garage.

When I was in Houston I heard of a cheap native who's still got the first million dollars he ever made.

One Texas oilman had a bankroll so big that he had to have it put on microfilm before he could stuff it in his wallet.

Sex

Sex makes the world go round. If Queen Isabella didn't dig Chris this world would still be square and ditto its inhabitants.

Down through the centuries, the subject of Sex has always been good for a laugh. That's not so surprising since Sex itself is pretty entertaining. Ever since Adam and Eve started the whole mess, there have been stories about it. I'm sure the gang that hung around with Romeo and Juliet, Tristan and Isolde, Napoleon and Josie, and Tommy Manville and anybody have made funny about the Boy and Girl problems.

Times have changed but the jokes linger on. In ye olden days when French kids studied anatomy, they went to college. Nowadays they enroll at Brigitte Bardot movies.

Mae West invited the gents in her audience to "come up and see me sometime." We even christened a life preserver after her. One comic said, "I bumped into Mae West this afternoon and she was across the street at the time." These howlers are handed down from one body to another as the new "Miss Mammary Gland" shows up. The big gag this year: "There will be a meeting of the big four—Dagmar and Jane Russell." When M.M. appeared on your favorite calendar, the line was "Marilyn is beautiful but it's only skin deep." The Jayne Mansfield joke, "She was wearing a house dress and there are no vacancies," was stolen from a Dagmarism. When one fan cracked to Gina Lallapalooza, "If I told you you had a beautiful body would you hold it against me?" she answered, "There's something I must get off my chest." "What is it?" he asked. "Your eyes."

"Anita Ekberg probably gets into a cab sideways," somebody resurrected from an old Jane Russellism, whilst another comic leered, "Monique Van Vooren makes my wife look like a boy."

Though Sex has been the basis for folks since Madame Pompadour, men know very little about women. There are two periods in a man's life when he doesn't know anything about women. Before marriage and after marriage. Consequently, I have engaged this planet's foremost expert on Love and Romance, Zsa Zsa Gabor, to settle some questions on the subject. Zsa and I have teamed together in night clubs for the past five years, and though Zsa Zsa and Joey Joey won't be immortalized in history as the hottest duo since Anthony and Cleopatra or even Abbott and Costello, she has been very enlightening on Zee Topic of L'amour. Nightly our audiences were invited to ask questions and here lie the answers exactly as they gushed from Zsa Zsa:

Q: Last night I stayed out all night with a man. Did I do wrong?
ZZ: You mean you don't remember?
Q: Do you think a girl should get married for love?
ZZ: Yes, and I think she should keep on getting married until she finds it.
Q: What is the difference between Parisian men and American men?
ZZ: Parisian men make love all day and have no time for work; American men work all day and have no time for love.
Q: Do you think that all women should have a mink?
ZZ: Why not? Every mink has one.
Q: But suppose her husband can't afford a mink coat?
ZZ: Then let him wear a trench coat.
Q: When a girl breaks off her engagement do you think it proper etiquette to return the ring?
ZZ: Yes, but I would keep the stone.
Q: When do you think is the right time for a girl to get married?
ZZ: Whenever she's single.
Q: When your mother got married a few years ago, did you approve?
ZZ: Of course—I think all mothers should be married.

Q: What kind of men do you like?

ZZ: I love the intellectual type, they know everything and suspect nothing.

Q: When you go out with a man are his intentions honorable or dishonorable?

ZZ: You mean I have a choice?

Q: What is your opinion of a diplomat?

ZZ: A diplomat is a man who always remembers a woman's birthday but never her age.

Q: What is your opinion of an ideal world?

ZZ: Where all the women are married and all the men are bachelors.

Q: What makes European men such sensational lovers?

ZZ: European women.

Q: What's the difference between Madame and Mademoiselle?

ZZ: Monsieur.

Q: What did you learn when you went to school as a child?

ZZ: I learned in school that money isn't everything. It's happiness that counts. So Momma sent me to a different school.

Q: Your mother had her own ideas about education?

ZZ: Yes. She always told me never to take diamonds from strangers.

Q: How about all those diamonds you're wearing?

ZZ: Joey, no one is perfect. She also told me when I get married to sleep only in a king-size bed—with a real king in it.

Q: You've been in this country for some time now. How do you like America?

ZZ: Oh Joey, I love everything about America. The people of America—the songs of America—the Bank of America.

Even Zig Zag admits she is no authority on Love and Romance. As she says, "Authority, look at my love life!" Look at it . . . a lot of guys would like to *be* it. Maybe she isn't an authority but she'll have to do until next year's sexpot comes along.

If these jokes seem to come from a woman hater, it's only that I hate to be without them—remember, Sex, according to old man Webster, is the difference between Men and

Women and as long as there is a Man and a Woman, they will have their differences. So here goes—out of the frying pan into the sexpot. . . .

The young man was making love to the starlet and said, "I don't have a lot of money like Aly Khan, I don't have expensive houses like Aly Khan and I can't afford a big diamond like Aly Khan, but I love you." "I love you, too," the starlet replied. "But tell me more about Aly Khan."

First Tourist: How long does it take you to go on a gondola ride?

Second Tourist: From ten minutes to three hours, depending on whether I'm with my wife or a pretty girl.

The new secretary was telling her employer about her last job. "If you must know," she explained, "my last boss fired me because of the mistake I wouldn't make."

A debutante is a girl whose life is one mad whirl of activity—day in and night out.

Guys who pinch pennies will never pinch chorus girls.

In Los Angeles, Sophia Loren went to see the Dodgers play. Before game time, she visited the Dodger dugout and chatted with Roy Campanella, the great catcher who's now a coach. "I always thought that if I were a man, I'd like to be a baseball catcher," she told Roy. An eavesdropper on the bench yelled out, "That's impossible, Baby, they don't make chest protectors that big!"

First starlet: How would you act if the producer made a pass at you?

Second starlet: In all the future pictures he'd make.

A beautiful broad visited the Bronx Zoo and asked where the monkeys were. "They're in the back making love," she was told. "Will they come out for peanuts?" she asked. "Would you?" the keeper inquired.

"I finally got my girl to say 'yes,'" he bragged. "When is the wedding?" his friend asked. "What wedding?"

The girl told her lawyer she wanted a divorce. "On what grounds?" "My husband isn't faithful." "What makes you think so?" asked the lawyer. "Well," she said, "I don't think he's the father of my child."

Did you ever notice when a girl tries on a sweater for the first time? She turns sideways to admire herself.

A smart female is one who quits playing ball when she makes a good catch.

Sex rears its ugly head in everything including sports. Racing—neck and neck; tennis—40 love; baseball—squeeze plays; hockey—body checks; football—making a pass.

Chorine to traffic cop: "Yes, I heard you whistle, officer, but I'd never get anywhere if I stopped every time anybody whistles at me."

Being bald has its advantages. When a bald man is on a sofa with a girl and her father walks in, all he has to do is straighten his tie.

It was their first date and they were both thinking of the same thing. She called it mental telepathy—he called it beginner's luck.

When the beau tried to get fresh with the flat-chested young girl, she screamed, "Here! Here!" He quickly replied, "Where? Where?"

This poor inert fellow was lying prostrate, face down, across the middle of a one-way street. When traffic was clogged up for miles, one sweet old lady clambered down off her Hupmobile, got down on all fours, sat astride the motionless body and began applying artifical respiration. Almost immediately there was a feeling of movement and the gent's head swiveled up to hers so that they faced on eyeball level. "Lissen, madam," the fellow said, "I don't know what game you're playing but I'm trying to repair these cables running under the street."

Then there's the one about the young sexy widow who lived alone but who had one peculiarity. When she paraded around the house, there was nothing covering the windows or the widow. Some nearsighted neighbors complained and the police paid her a visit. Sure enough, she was as naked as the truth, except for a pair of pearl earrings.

"How come you're not wearing any clothing?" asked the police officer happily.

"I don't need any," she said. "I never have any company."

"Oh yeah?" questioned the drooling cop suspiciously, "then why are you wearing them earrings?"

"Well, *somebody* might drop in."

At the senior prom a fresh young freshman sidled up to the gorgeous sloe-eyed beauty and threw her a glance. When she didn't pick it up, he asked her for a dance. The girl honored him with a frosty glare. "I never dance with a child." Peering closely at her he apologized, "I'm sorry, I didn't realize your condition."

The twelve-year-old hillbilly from the mountains of Tennessee was built like the mountains of Tennessee. The barefooted, bare-armed girl hightailed it down to her boy friend's shack and shoved a brand-new baby at him. "Hyar," she said angrily, "he's yourn and tha'ss the last time I'll ever listen to you. Y'all said we wuz only wrestling."

So this here fellow put his foot on the brake and his hand on the girl and whispered, "What do you say, Margie?" She thought a full half a second. "Okay, but remember you talked me into it."

The traveling salesman had to write his report to the company but he had no writing paper so he popped by the town's greeting card store. "Greetings," said the salesman to the saleslady, whose neckline was sliced to her hemline. "Do you keep stationery?" "Yes I do, right up until the last second—than I go simply wild."

The patient was so thrilled because the psychiatrist helped her that she bubbled. Leaning over, she cooed to the headman, "Oh, doctor, you've made me so happy I could hug you." The psychiatrist cautioned her, "You'd better not. Actually, we shouldn't even be lying on the couch together."

Whether you're rich or poor it's always good to have sex. So, this poor beggar with his body all achin' and racked with pain, hobbles up to me, palm outstretched, and wheezes, "Say pal, how's about a quarter for coffee?" "Coffee's only a dime," I says. "I'm keeping a woman," he says.

With the city traffic problem so acute, many a New York businessman is hard put to take care of all his affairs. The other lunchtime, one executive dashed into his ladyfriend's midtown hotel and hysterically began smothering her with kisses. "Easy does it, lover boy," she said, "relax. A Rossano Brazzi you're not! Romance me a little." "I have to hurry, honey," he gasped, "I'm double-parked."

I've seen a lot of beauties from all over the world, but of all of them, I'd say Esther Williams is really worth wading for.

A Harvard bird came a-visiting his chickadee, only to discover she was crying up a river. The girl was sobbing and slobbering and the bright lad decided to find out what's wrong. "What's wrong?" he said. "Well," she cried, "Malcolm said I was a ——" Knowing how dreadfully Harvard this fellow was, she spelled the offensive word so as not to upset him. A look of pain came over the Bostonian. His patrician nostrils flared and his artistic face paled. Clearly he was hurt and anguished. "No, no, Pamela, it's spelled with a W."

Russia

Laughter is one commodity that has never been exported from Russia. What have they got to laugh about? Khrushchev may be funny to us but to them it's no laughing matter.

Russia has so much censorship you can't even sneak out caviar today. Over there even the fish are afraid to open their mouths. The sign in the voting booth reads VOTE COMMUNIST —THE LIFE YOU SAVE MAY BE YOUR OWN.

One couple was ankling along the street minding their own business. "You know," Ivan whispered to his wife, "I have the funniest feeling we're not being followed."

In the Soviet nobody dares throw eggs at men like Mikoyan. The starving people would rather eat them.

Their favorite quiz show is *I've Got A Secret Police*. First prize is two tickets to an execution.

A Muscovite entered his local police station and reported that his parrot was missing. "Does your parrot talk?" asked the man in charge. "Oh, yes," answered the frightened comrade, "but any political opinions he expresses are strictly his own."

One sober day, when Khrushchev was reviewing the troops, he beckoned to one little soldier and asked, "How is everything?" The boy answered, "I can't complain." "You bet your life you can't," answered Khrushchev.

This gives you a slight idea of the job I had smuggling these jokes out of the USSR. Black market gags are as tough to get out of the gagged Russians as it is for the people themselves to lam out of the Soviet. A case in point is the tale of the Moscow University professor who told his class that interplanetary junketing was distinctly in the cards. "We will be able to travel to Mars, Pluto and Venus," the savant said. "Are there any questions?" A student in the back of the lecture hall raised his hand. "When," he asked, "can we travel to Vienna?"

One Russian was found to be physically equipped to survive the first rocket to the moon but he refused to make the trip. The commissar insisted. "Don't you like to travel?" "Sure!" said the comrade, "but not to the moon." The commissar questioned, "Then where would you like to travel?" "To America," he answered. "We can only take you to the moon," said the commissar. "If we could go to America, I'd go myself."

When Stalin died, millions of people went to the funeral. "How come so many people turned out?" asked a visitor. "I thought everybody hated him." "Oh," said a mourner, "just give the people what they want."

One sick Russky was in bed in the middle of the night when a knock came on the door. "Who is it?" he demanded. "The Angel of Death," came the reply. "Thank goodness," said the comrade, "I was afraid it was the Secret Police."

A Soviet citizen died and found himself in the suburbs of hell. The demon in charge of admissions asked him whether he wanted to use the Capitalist or the Communist entrance to the sepulchral world of perdition. "The Communist one, of course," the shrewd fellow replied promptly, "there's bound to be a fuel shortage in that sector."

The Russians expect to reach the moon this year, Mars next year, and by 1975 they expect every Russian will own a pair of shoes.

A Muscovite was convicted of having called the Minister of Culture a fool. He got a 20-year sentence—5 years for slander and 15 for revealing a State secret.

The important Russian commissar lay in an oxygen tent and felt that he was going fast. Weakly, he whispered to his chief assistant, "Ivan, I only have a few minutes left. I want you to know I'm leaving you everything—my house, my farm, my electric heater, even my mistress. Ivan, everything goes to you. All I ask from you in return is one last favor." The assistant exclaimed eagerly, "Yes, yes, Commissar. Anything, anything at all. What is it?" Feebly, the dying man murmured, "Please take your foot off the oxygen tube."

In Leningrad an old man sat on a park bench and dozed. When he awoke he noticed two uniformed policemen sitting on either side of him. "My God!" he mumbled. "What did I dream?"

When Bob Hope visited Russia he quipped, "This is the only country in the world where television watches you." Hope said he saw the Soviet leader on television. "Of course it's easy for Khrushchev to be a hit on TV—all his critics are in Siberia," cracked Bob. Jack Benny was annoyed at Ski-nose copping so much publicity about his trip to Russia. "What's the big deal," jabbed Benny. "I went to Russia, visited my family and came home."

My secret underground-joke spy informs me there's a sign in every government official's office which carries this legend: HEAD UP AS LONG AS YOU HAVE ONE.

An American visitor was trying out his transistor radio on a Soviet train. Seated nearby was a Russian unable to contain his curiosity. But, patriotically, he phrased it this way: "We have those too," he said, and added, "What is it?"

When the Russians heard we name cigarettes after towns like Newport, Winston and Salem, they decided to come out with the Siberia. It's the cigarette with the salt mine flavor and it's so strong that when the smoke gets in your eyes you start blinking . . . it's sort of a blinking man's cigarette.

The Russians know nothing about interior decorating. Why would anybody with good taste prefer an iron curtain to Venetian blinds?

After spending twenty years in the United States, a man returned to his birthplace, Russia. He had heard many stories about the New Russia so he left his wife and three-year-old son Karl behind and promised to let them know the true conditions in his native land. Soon after, his wife received a letter: *Russia is as wonderful as ever. I'm very happy here and I want you to come over as soon as you can. But of course, not until after Karl's wedding.*

Two comrades were talking about their jobs in their respective factories. "We manufacture baby carriages," one said. "That's wonderful," replied the second, "my wife just had a baby. I wonder if you can get me one." "Why certainly," answered his friend, "but we only manufacture single parts so you'll have to assemble it yourself." The new father got his parts and a few days later he ran into his friend, who asked him if he had any trouble assembling the parts. "No," answered the father, "but the carriage is no use to me. It looks and shoots like a machine gun."

Two former Russian generals met in a Siberian camp. "Comrade," said one, "in me you behold an ex-general of the Red Army who never took an order from Khrushchev." "That's odd," replied the second. "In me you behold an ex-general of the Red Army who obeyed every single Khrushchev command."

The story is told of the Communist who died and went to hell. Upon his arrival, he told Satan, "Boy, am I happy to be in heaven." "But you're mistaken," the devil told him, "this isn't heaven." "That's what you think," sighed the comrade. "I just came from Siberia."

As is so often the case, the commissar of a small Russian town had lost favor with Comrade Khrushchev and was sentenced to be executed. Before he was taken to the firing squad, a guard said, "I bet all your enemies will be happy to see you die!" The condemned one smiled and slowly said, "What enemies? I had them all shot a long time ago!"

I have one suggestion to cement better laugh relations between the USSR and the USA. When Khrushchev comes to America, we ought to give him a 21-gun salute—and aim the guns right at him.

Russia is where you are allowed to go anywhere they please.

The teacher tells the principal that one of her lads is "a year ahead of everybody else." The principal gives the lad a brief test. "Name the three greatest traitors in Russian history," he demands. "Stalin, Beria and Khrushchev" announces the kid. The principal turns in amazement to the teacher. "Y'know something," he said, "he *is* a year ahead of everybody else."

A traveler came back this year from Stalingrad and claimed he saw a sign warning, in a secret church, reading, IN PRAYING HERE, YOU KEEP YOUR EYES CLOSED AT YOUR OWN RISK.

Asked whether gum is manufactured in the Soviet Union, a Russian grins and replies, "No, we Communists consider that to chew without swallowing is unproductive."

The newspaper *Pravda* is running a contest for the best political joke. First prize—20 years.

Lenin is supposed to have remarked that there could be any number of political parties in the Soviet Union but only on one condition—the Communist Party must be in power and all the other parties must be in jail.

All foreigners in Russia fear that microphones are hidden in their bedrooms. The fiancée of a diplomat became so worried about this invasion of privacy that she consulted a psychiatrist. "I'd suggest," said the practical doctor, "that when you make love, you simply do so quietly."

A Soviet dignitary returned from Copenhagen and reported that economic conditions were very bad in Denmark. Surprised, one listener pointed out that Danish store windows were full of goods. "Oh, yes," conceded the Communist, "but the Danish people have no money to buy. There were no lines in front of the stores."

This is a typical Russian couple living as the Russian government expects them to live:

SASCHA: I'm depressed. I worked eighteen hours today.

MASHA: Don't complain, a part-time job is better than nothing.

SASCHA: I'm going to watch television. My favorite quiz program, *I Was In the FBI for the Communist Party,* is on.

MASHA: You'll watch all night and there goes our making love.

SASCHA: Making love, bah! How can a man make love when he lives in the same apartment with twelve other people?

MASHA: But Sascha, it didn't bother you last night.

SASCHA: Last night...I wasn't even home last night.

MASHA: I hope it was a Party member.

SASCHA: Me, too. Otherwise I could get into trouble with my Leader. Remember, there's a quota on making love. Our Leader allows us five every month and we've used up our quota.

MASHA: So, I'll borrow Mama's quota. She hasn't been using it lately.

SASCHA: Tell me, how many children have we had since we were married?

MASHA: Five.

SASCHA: Only five? We did better than that when we were single.

MASHA: Sascha, you forget one thing. My father is a commissar and if my husband doesn't make me happy—it's Siberia.

SASCHA: I-yi-yi, how many of your husbands are in Siberia right now?

MASHA: Six—Father sent two and the other four bought their own tickets.

SASCHA: In that case I follow my Leader. Come, my little shashlik, and I'll show you what I can do.

MASHA: You may not realize it, but today you're really following your Leader.

A Hollywood producer who had returned to his native St. Petersburg for a visit was summoned to Moscow by the Commissar of Culture. "Comrade," said the Commissar, "you're a great producer and I have chosen you to produce an epic film about our glorious revolution. It will show all the great leaders of our country; our soldiers, our peasants

and even our slaves. It'll have a cast of over 250,000 people."
"But that'll cost a fortune," the producer interrupted, "do
you realize how many rubles it'll cost to hire all those extras?"
"Rubles, nothing!" barked the Commissar. "Who uses extras?
In this country we believe in realism. When we want to use
slaves in pictures we put in a call to Siberia and get real
ones!"

A reporter from a Kremlin weekly went to Khrushchev's
headquarters to interview him. When he returned to his office,
his editor asked, "And what did our wonderful Leader say
today?" "He didn't say a thing," the reporter answered, "he
had to rush off to a conference and told me to come back
tomorrow." "In that case," smiled the editor, "keep the story
down to just the front page."

And so, this ends Russia ... which wouldn't be a bad
idea altogether.

Hollywood

Hollywood is a small town bordered on the north by producers, on the south by starlets, on the west by producers'
wives and on the east by ulcers. Movie producers are normal
men with abnormal schemes, subnormal wallets and over-
active sex glands. Their brains are stuffed with figures,
blondes and brunettes—both financial and female. Oscar after
Oscar they plod through thick and thin, tortured by visions
of their idols—De Mille, Sam Goldwyn and Errol Flynn.

Mommies, attempting to discover what makes an ordinary,
happy, carefree cad become a motion picture producer, ask
"Where did he go wrong?" If in infancy he grabs for the
nurse instead of the bottle and if in kindergarten his favorite
story is "Little Red Riding Hood," and if in high school he
makes the dramatic class—the whole dramatic class—these are
danger signals. Artistically, he's fertile and creative, often
producing two epics and three kids a year and is the back-
bone of Hollywood's main industry. Many a starlet readily
admits, quote: "I owe everything to my first producer who
made me." End of quote.

And what is a starlet? My dictionary defines starlets thusly:

Young actresses who are being promoted for the purpose of leading roles in motion pictures. Figures—whaddaya expect from two squares named Funk & Wagnall. The only correct segment propounded by Messrs. Wagnall and/or Funk is that she's young and being promoted. Into what, by *whom,* even Webster doesn't say. As she progresses from B pictures to A pictures to AA we read that Sadie Blintzas, that shy, naïve, homespun babe from Pasteurpile, New Mexico, now has two sequin Cadillacs, an indoor ranch with a hot and cold running butler and is, today, Nelga Stacey the M-G-M sexbox.

Unfortunately, not every hopeful becomes successful in the Hollywoods; some fall by the wayside or in other motels because of ruinous faults like strict morals or a small bustline or that dread characteristic which panics moviedom—talent.

Like this Hollywood producer who hesitated at offering a once-famous movie actress a part in his newest picture. "Darling," he darlinged the star, "you may not want to play this role. It calls for a lovely but immoral prostitute who runs from the arms of one man to another . . . a woman who lies and cheats . . . a woman engulfed in reckless passion . . . a real witch. . . . Tell me, how do you feel about it?" "Feel about it?" the actress sighed. "It's the first decent part I've been offered in years!"

Comedian Marty Allen tells of the Hollywood schoolboy who asked his teacher for a larger report card, explaining, "I'd like to get *all* my parents to sign it!"

Did you hear about the very sentimental Hollywood star who wanted to get divorced in the same dress in which her mother got divorced?

A producer had bought a play from an unknown writer for an unheard-of sum. He handed it to a talented director and instructed, "Read it, and then we'll make an Academy Award winner." The director read the script and when he came back to the producer he was white as a sheet. "Sir, we can't make this story. It's about a Lesbian." He waited for the boss to start screaming, but the producer maintained his calm. "In that case," shrugged the producer, "just make her some other nationality."

The wife of one of those "method" actors went to a psychiatrist and told him, "Doctor, my husband thinks he's Marlon Brando." "Why do you say that?" asked the head shrinker. "Because all day long he hangs around the house and rips up his undershirts."

Two actors met at Hollywood and Vine. The first had his bags packed and appeared to be hurrying out of town. "Where you going?" asked his friend. "I thought you were starting work on a new picture." "Well, it's like this," explained the departing one. "Do you remember that pretty starlet I was dating?" "You mean that redhead?" "Well, yesterday she gave birth to a boy, and I'm—" "Say no more," his friend sighed sympathetically. "I guess yours is just a case of Had Son . . . Must Travel."

Two actors met on Sunset Boulevard and one mentioned he had just landed his first TV job. "That's wonderful," smiled his friend, "what part do you play? The cowboy or the Indian?"

En route to an acting class, the two starlets in off-the-shoulder dungarees bumped into each other (and they were across the street at the time). One said, "I had a terrible nightmare last night. I dreamt that Eddie Fisher had his hands around me and was squeezing real tight." "I don't see anything so terrible about that," squealed her friend. "Eddie's a very charming fellow." "Yeah," sighed the other, "but in my dream I was Debbie Reynolds."

Director: She reminds me of Jayne Mansfield.
Producer: Why is that?
Director: Because she'd walk a mile for a camera.

There are so many of those foreign sports cars in California that half the drivers out there are getting their licenses from the Berlitz language school.

There's a hotel in Hollywood so ritzy that even the mousetraps have adjoining baths.

A movieland wife, explaining why she was divorcing her current husband, explained, "I always thought we were perfectly mated until one night the TV set broke down and we had a chance to talk."

So these Hollywood kiddies were playing house. Said one: "We're going to have a big family—I want three fathers and three mothers."

There are plenty of happy Hollywood marriages—and most of them take place in the movies filmed there. Which reminds us of the much-married Hollywood babe, who was described as a good housekeeper—"with every settlement she keeps the house!"

A Hollywood marriage is a good way to spend a weekend.

So many things are a sham in Hollywood. Many girls have false hair, false eyebrows, they wear falsies and false teeth; the men have their shoulders built up and they wear toupees. So when you see two stars on the screen, it's not two people making love, it's just a lot of commodities getting together.

Hollywood is where the people accept you for what you're *not*.

It isn't that I don't like the people in Hollywood; it's just that I don't like the Hollywood in people.

Hollywood people are really lucky. Can you imagine if they had to pay taxes on the money they claim they make?

In Hollywood, a silver wedding anniversary means the 25th husband.

In Hollywood when they invite you to a party, their invitations read *Admit Bearer and one wife.*

In Hollywood there's a 16-inch difference between a pat on the back and a kick in the pants.

Hollywood is where the wedding cake outlasts the wedding.

When a Hollywood bride walked into her new home, she turned to her new husband and said, "Jack, darling, this house looks familiar. Are you sure we haven't been married before?"

In Hollywood he'd be a movie mogul . . . in China, he's a big movie Mongolian!

When I first went to Hollywood I was such a square, I went to motels and I slept in them.

A Hollywood romance in 4 acts: Act 1—their eyes meet
                                 Act 2—their lips meet
                                 Act 3—their souls meet
                                 Act 4—their lawyers meet!

Hollywood is where they take you for better or for worse, but not for good.

In Hollywood, marriage is sufficient grounds for divorce.

In Hollywood, a jewelry shop advertises *Wedding Bands for 98c guaranteed not to tarnish for 6 months.*

I know one actor in Hollywood who's got a home where the kitchen alone has five rooms.

In Hollywood an actor is getting old when he goes away on a vacation instead of a honeymoon.

In Hollywood they don't ask "How's your wife," they say "Who's your wife!" Hollywood is making a new picture called *Boom and Bust.* I don't know whether it's about our current times or the development of the H-bomb starring Jayne Mansfield.

The official Hollywood drink—Marriage on the rocks!

Two agents met on a Hollywood street and one said, "Hey, what are you so down in the mouth for?" His friend said, "It's that new client of mine. How would you like to represent a client that sings like Crosby, wiggles like Presley, fights like John Wayne and acts like Marlon Brando?" His friend said, "Are you screwy? Why, you'll make a million bucks with a guy like that!" and the other agent said, "Guy nothing, ya dope, it's a girl!"

Many stories come out of Hollywood: Groucho Marx once invited Oscar Levant to his home for dinner and Levant accepted. Groucho said, "Could you make it Saturday?" and Levant said it was fine. Groucho said, "Come about seven, we'll have a couple of cocktails first and then we'll sit down to a luscious New York cut steak that our cook can prepare to perfection. We'll have some of our favorite wine and some gorgeous out-of-the world dessert." Levant went wild and said, "Gee, Groucho, that all sounds great, tell me—what's your address?" and Groucho said, "Ha! Wouldn't ya like to know?"

CHAPTER 4

THE ADAMS DAILY
DOZEN

THINKING funny is a twenty-four-hour-seven-day-a-week job and you can't strike for shorter hours. Whoever heard of a comedian who's only funny on Thursday? You have to think funny whether you feel it or not. If you're sad, think of sad jokes—"if it rained soup I'd be standing in the street with a fork"; if you're sick, think of illness jokes—"I took a four-way cold tablet but it didn't know which way to go." You must keep thinking! My friends always say, "There goes Joey Adams, that thinker." At least that's what they say they say. For "thinking-funny" exercises take your average day and pick out things, any things, and try to make jokes about them. Just regard your brain as a thinking man's filter that sifts the humor out of life. Here's a typical thinking-funny exercise you could use. It's called the *Daily Dozen* exercises for the humor muscles in your skull, guaranteed not to cramp your funny bone or give you a mental hernia.

Daily Dozen

You get up in the morning and you brush your teeth. Let's see, a brushing teeth gag.

(1) "I wonder if the French kiss will ever replace the toothbrush."

You eat a big breakfast, so how about an egg joke?

(2) "It was so windy in Iowa, a hen laid the same egg twelve times."

You then get on the train to go to work.

(3) I asked the conductor on the train if he could run any faster. "Yeah," he said, "but I gotta stay in the train."

You finally arrive at work, but you're a little late.

(4) "Sorry I'm late, boss, but my socks are guaranteed not to run."

Ah, eventually it's time for your coffee break.

(5) "My wife soaked her evening dress in coffee so it would stay up all night."

Sitting in the office, you glance out the window and comment on the weather.

(6) "It was so hot in Florida that the palms were sweating."

Then you go to lunch at a fancy restaurant.

(7) "I impressed my friends. I ordered the whole meal in French—which shook up the waiter, as it was a Chinese restaurant."

Back to the job and you begin to get a little tired doing the same thing all day.

(8) "I'd like a new job, like my brother—he's a life guard in a car wash."

Finally, late in the day, you have that quick one for the road.

(9) "Well, they redecorated my favorite bar—they put new drunks around it."

Then home to the wife (preferably your own) for that great home cooking of hers.

(10) "My wife's some cook. She can't even make ice cubes. She's the only woman I know who can louse up corn flakes."

After dinner, settle down and watch TV for a while.

(11) "I watch TV all the time. Last night I turned on the radio by mistake and thought I'd gone blind."

And now it's finally time to go to bed, and if you're married and this is where you think up your jokes—good luck to you! But ...

(12) "If you want to drive your wife crazy, don't talk in your sleep—just grin."

After accumulating some gags, try them out on your friends. Don't worry about telling the same story twice to the same friend. After you lose your friends, start telling them to your relatives, you have nothing to lose there. If possible, try the same gag on different types of people, such as fat accountants, skinny professors, busy bus drivers, idle presidents, etc. Watch their responses: where did each laugh? not laugh? walk away? kick you? Obey the #1 rule: ANNOY PEOPLE.

PART 3

CHAPTER 1

SOME OF MY BEST
FRIENDS ARE JOKES

OLD jokes never die, they just end up in every comic's brain file. Like a well-aimed kick in the derrière, a gag can only be effective if it's sent in the right direction, at the right target. But in order to bull's-eye, you must have plenty of ammunition and that's why it's so important to have a big store of lethal lines ready.

If you wanna be the life of the party, don't be caught with your gags down or your laughs open.

You never know when or where your best yocks will be found or stolen. I have been circled and cornered by squares from the Halls of Montezuma to the Shores of Coney Island, who insist "this is the funniest." It's usually a joke from one of my own books or from one of my club acts, that I discarded long ago. Don't misunderstand me, some of my best friends are jokes. I have received the greatest array of comedy material from pals all over the country. Naturally every joke you hear isn't usable, but it takes patience to find that diamond in the roughneck. Once you let your friends know you're shopping for material, life will become one big supermarket of gags. Just get everyone conditioned and all you have to do is ring the bell and they'll start "salvo-ing" jokes all over you. So listen carefully as your friends try to make funny. I did and I'm considered the guy with the best "ear" in the business, maybe not the best act, but the best ear.

Everyone says they love to hear me listen. I can't understand what they mean by that.

The friends that feed me jokes have been doctors, lawyers and Indian chiefs, and their funny bones have been hitting me on the head for years. My pal Leonard Simons, the advertising biggie of Detroit, is a very influential man in his business as well as a great philanthropist, but at home he claims, "Being a husband is like any other job—it's easier if you like your boss."

His partner, Larry Michelson says, "How can I tell my wife her hair looks like a mop? She doesn't know what a mop is."

Lyn Durant is one of the world's great mechanical minds. In his Chicago office, jokes flow as easily as the liquor. Lyn told me about "the auto mechanic who went to a psychiatrist and from force of habit climbed under the couch."

Morton Edell, prex of Lanolin Plus and Rybutol (who has the healthiest hair in the world), told me about a diet-conscious lady he knows who once weighed 180 pounds, but now weighs only 85 pounds . . . casket and all.

Ralph Schneider, head of Diners' Club, is an old pal who never lets me by without listening to a selection from his gag menu. He told me about the two Irishmen passing a restaurant that advertised kosher food. One said, "What's that sign mean?" The other replied, "To you it means nothing, to me it means nothing, but to the Jewish people, that's Duncan Hines."

After filling up with tasties from Ralph, I smacked into an old and close friend, Harry Sylk, boss of Consolidated Sun Ray, who's usually playing with stocks. He's always helped me do well in the market, as he put it, "until his shopping bag broke and the bottom fell out."

I'm always assured of an entree of gags when I make the rounds of the New York dining spots. These guys probably have a better file of one-liners than most comedians. At Danny's Hideaway, Tara Pozzi sits on the throne as princess, where she, her Uncle Danny, and her father, Dalmo, reign.

Tara told me about the deep-sea diver who got the message, "Come up quick. The ship is sinking!"

At The Harwyn, Ed Wynn, the owner, served me up this appetizer. "A cannibal walked in here the other night and ordered a waiter."

Before I was eaten alive by the rest of his one-liners, I visited my friend Vito Pisa, at the Chez Vito, who said, "I got a brother-in-law who is so lazy that he gets in a revolving door and waits."

Sal Cucinotta at Teddy's pounced on me with his joke for the evening. Sal told me about the fella whose new Italian sports car was so low that he didn't get into it—he put it on!

At the Spindletop, Joe Marsh told me about the nudist who was so strict he wouldn't even allow dressing on his sandwich.

The night got shorter, but the jokes longer as I stopped in at Leone's to see Gene Leone, who seated me with this one: "I know a guy who's really flabby. In fact, he's got so many double chins he needs a bookmark to find his collar."

I figured I was able to digest about one more gag, so I ended the evening at the East Side La Strada, where the Rose Brothers gave me my "dessert." They said, "Joey, you've been so nice to us, we really don't deserve a person like you . . . then again, we don't deserve sinus trouble either but we got it." For that gag I gave them a big hand . . . right across the mouth.

So you see, just hang around saloons where people congregate and you're bound to pick up some material along with some expensive bills. Hotels are also good listening grounds. Just be sure the house detective doesn't catch you stealing more than gags.

Like Dick Flannagan, the veep with the Zeckendorf hotel chain, said to me on one stay, "Did you hear about the drunk who was driving his car the wrong way down a one-way street? The cop stopped him and said, 'Where are you going?' The drunk answered, 'I don't know but I must be late, 'cause everybody else is coming back.' "

Paul Grossinger of the famous Grossinger resort threw this

one at me one time. "I was going to have water-polo games for my guests this summer. But during the very first game three horses drowned."

And every time I decorate the Virgin Isle Hotel, Henry Kimmelman is sure to come up with a gemeroo like the guy who went to the psychiatrist complaining, "I have the most horrible dream every night. I dream I come to this door with a big sign on it and I push and I push and I can't get in." "What's the sign say?" said the psychiatrist. "Pull," he answered.

Last time I was down at the Roosevelt in New Orleans, Seymour Weiss gave me this one. A lady got on a train in New York and asked the conductor "Does this train stop at San Francisco?" He said, "It better, lady, or there's gonna be a hell of a splash!"

And Alan Schafer, owner of the South of the Border Motel, "The Waldorf of the Road," in Dillon, South Carolina, told about a woman he knew who was so rich she had four Cadillacs. One for each direction . . .

Before I can open my mouth somebody's usually shoving a gag down it. Like when I visited Porter Stiles, Miguel Pombo and Guillermo Uribe of the Avianca Airline. A passenger making reservations handed me the story about the little old lady who got on a plane for the first time and complained her ears felt funny. The stewardess gave her some Chiclets and said they would help. When they landed, the stewardess asked if that had alleviated the popping. The little old lady replied, "Yes, it certainly did, but it was pretty messy trying to get the gum out of my ears."

People tell me jokes in every town . . . Los Angeles, Chicago, New York, New Haven & Hartford. Take Detroit. (Now there's an offer.) Sashaying I go down the street in Detroit and this is what happens—

Nate S. Shapero, Chairman of the Board of the Cunningham Drug Company, stops me with: A lady walked into a luncheonette-type drugstore, and said, "Do you fit men's trusses here?" "Yes," said the clerk. "Well wash your hands then, I want a chocolate soda," snapped the woman.

Then Max Fisher, Chairman of the Board of Aurora Gasoline Company, yells out his office window, "Hey Joey, hear about the crosseyed schoolteacher who couldn't keep her pupils under control."

Abner Wolf of ACF Wrigleys shouts from a passing car—which almost hits me—"Don't worry, Joey, this guy driving can't see so well, but he's so rich he's got prescription windshields."

I turn a corner and bump into Lou Elliman, president of the Elliman Steel Company, who says, "Never rob a Chinese bank. Because an hour later you want to rob another one."

Paul Zukerman, vice-prexy of the Sunshine Biscuit Company, taps me on the shoulder and says, "I knew a fellow who was so shy he pulled down the shades every time he changed his mind."

Jules Shubot, the jeweler, steps out of his store to polish off this little diamond: A guy went to a psychiatrist and said, "Doc, don't waste my time. I got two questions. Just answer them. First, could I possibly be in love with an elephant?"

"Of course not," said the Doc. "Now what's the other question?"

"Where can I get rid of a rather large engagement ring?"

Harry Hirsch, President of the Hall Lamp Company, shouts from across the street, "Hey Joey, I passed my eye test and got my driver's license."

"Was it tough?" I shout back.

"Not very. They told me to put my hand over my eye and count my fingers."

Alfred Epstein, President of the Pfeiffer Brewing Company, waves, smiles and says, "I'm on my way to the dentist. I've got so many cavities, I talk with an echo."

The President of Arrow Liqueurs Corporation, Tommy McMasters, stops me long enough to knock me out with this: Two little kids were standing on the street and a little girl went by. "Her neck's dirty," said one. "Her does?" said the other.

Just as I'm helping a little old lady of 22 across the street, Maurey "Santa Claus" Aronson, of the Aronson Printing

Company, slips a little piece of paper in my pocket. It reads *Definition of a sadist. A guy who does nice things for a masochist.*

Roy Dossin, a Detroit Pepsi-Cola bottler, catches me on the other side of the street with, "Doctor, all night I walk in my sleep." The doctor replies, "Ah, you're an insomniac." "No, I'm a night watchman."

Bernie Aronson, the stockbroker, punched home with this one: "Hello, landlord, my whole house is flooded with water." The landlord sarcastically says, "What d'ya expect for twenty dollars a month, champagne?"

Detroit insurance man Sid Bertin tips his hat and drops this one:

"Doctor, come quickly. My husband has swallowed a fountain pen."

"I'll be right over. What are you doing in the meantime?"

"Using a pencil."

Joe Mellon, the Detroit yachtsman, swears he overheard this at the club. One young gal said to the other, "He not only lied about the size of his yacht—he made me row."

Elwood Kukes of the Michigan Nut and Bolt Company breezes by with "A successful executive is a man with two desks—one for each foot."

A Detroit real estate friend, Chuck Gershenson, tells the one about the one-fingered pickpocket who stole Lifesavers.

And Harry Jacobson, the big Stainless Steel man in Detroit, catches me with "I got a cousin who had a birthday and received thirty pairs of cuff links. And you know, he hasn't got one shirt with French cuffs."

"What'd he do?" I asked.

"Got his wrists pierced."

By just walking down the street in Detroit I got one blonde in my eye and 12 jokes.

Today's big businessmen are making a bigger business out of making funny. Instead of stocks, they're trading in yocks. No matter what line they're in, they all have a drawerful of one-liners. And I always seem to catch them with their drawers open.

Bill Baybrooks of Gulf Oil, a good friend, drilled me with this one: "Did you hear about the guy who got a divorce and got custody of his wife's parents?"

The big building and construction man, Stanley Broff, told me about the tough neighborhood he hailed from. "It was so tough that a cat with a tail was considered a tourist and we used to play games like spin the cop."

William Black, who heads Chock Full o' Nuts, is always chock full of jokes. He slipped me the one about the drunk who, after leaving a wild party, was staggering home. He decided to take a short cut through the cemetery. Unfortunately, he fell into an open grave. He lay there for a while, getting very cold, when suddenly he heard footsteps. Another drunk was walking home the same way. The drunk in the grave yelled, "Hey, up there, help me, I'm freezing." The other drunk replied, "No wonder," and started to kick dirt down into the open grave.

Colonel Henschell, of Bulova Watches, wound up with this 17-jewel line: "I know a guy who's a great magician. He can walk down the street and turn into a saloon."

Meyer Robinson, my buddy with Manischewitz Wine, let me savor one of his vintage jokes: about the pretty Catholic girl who wanted to marry a nice Jewish boy. The mother of the girl told her daughter, "If he loves you he'll become a good Catholic. Talk to him, convince him of the great things about the Catholic religion. You're a good talker, honey, you can do it." So she talked and talked to her boyfriend and finally everything was going right. They had even set a wedding date, until one day the girl came home crying and said, "We're not getting married." "But why?" said the mother. "I thought he was convinced of our faith after you talked to him." Her daughter tearfully replied, "That's just it, Mom. I talked to him, but I talked too good—now he's going to be a priest."

Charles Meltzer, who's in ladies' blouses (don't tell his wife), believes in the philosophy that women's clothes should be like barbed wire . . . protect the property without obstructing the view.

Well, that's the way to get your jokes...it's also the way to hold your friends. To gather dribbles here and drabbles there, just wander amongst the rank and file. Lots of what you'll hear is rank and most of it you already got in the files—but just keep your friends feeding you. Remember, a comic never gets overweight from too much material. My advice is: walk around with your eyes open and your ear to the ground and if you don't end up a good comic at least you'll be a helluvan acrobat.

I've been told that my books are the kind you can't put down, mostly because of the glue on the binding. So, read on, and if you ever write a book I'll read this far for you....

CHAPTER 2

JOEY'S PORTABLE GAG FILE

IF you've ever watched kiddies playing with their ABC building blocks, you're hep to what comedians look like playing with their ABCs of yocks. These grown-up kiddies play, piling up the right gags, building columns of jokes, cementing routines, stacking up the laughs and, if successful, by the time they're in that Second Childhood they're still playing with building blocks . . . only now the blocks they're building on are 5th Avenue and Park Avenue.

In the following pages I've alphabetized many different types of jokes, from A to Z, according to subject. If you get in the habit of doing this it will be easier to find the right jokes at the right time. . . . And you'll also get to know the alphabet better. . . .

A Is for Africa: I was rather disappointed with the pictures I took in Africa of the native women . . . they weren't very well developed.

Africa is known as "Texas with Arabs."

They've educated the Ubangis in Africa to work. Some of them work for the Post Office sealing envelopes after they're dropped in the mailbox.

In Africa, the savage tribes pay no taxes. Then what makes them savage?

A Is for Art:

One day while I was in the jungle, a lion came so close to me I could feel his breath on the back of my neck, so what do I do? I turned up my collar.

A cannibal—that's a guy who loves his fellowman—with gravy!

Two Ubangi girls met one very hot day in the jungle and one of them stuck her face right up close to the other one's face and rapidly knocked off *"Peter Piper Picked a Peck of Pickled Peppers.* Now you fan me a while."

A Is for Agent: An agent submitted the name of his singer client to Rodgers and Hammerstein for a role in the film version of *Oklahoma.* Dick Rodgers heard the client's name and told the agent she wouldn't do. "We saw her for *Me and Juliet,"* he said. "The girl we're looking for must be five foot one. Your client is at least five foot eight." . . . The agent sat back, smiled and said, "But have you seen her lately?"

A Is for Analysis: I realized after four years and $10,000 worth of analysis that if I'd had the $10,000 in the first place, I wouldn't have needed the analysis.

A Is for Animals: This involves a famous dog trainer who gave a party in honor of his talented Alsatian. As part of the entertainment, the hound lumbered over to the baby grand, climbed onto the stool and proceeded to play a Bach sonata. Halfway through, one of the guests spoke too loudly and the animal growled and chased his heckler into a neutral corner. "Don't worry," the dog's trainer shouted, "his Bach is worse than his bite!"

A Is for Antiques: When the wife came home with her arms loaded with antiques, the husband commented: "I'm amazed to see all the things you would rather have than money."

One way to get rich is to be able to determine when a piece of junk becomes an antique.

A Is for Arabia: In Arabia I understand that a girl is proposed to by at least a dozen men who get down on their knees all at one time. Then she chooses one and the rest stay on their knees and wind up the occasion with the damndest crap game you ever saw.

A Is for Art: An art collector spotted an ad in the paper for a Van Gogh for $250. Although he was positive it was a misprint, he rushed over to the address listed in the ad. "It's no mistake," said the lady who had placed the ad, "it's a genuine Van Gogh." The collector quickly made out a check and bought the painting. "I don't get it, lady," he questioned after the sale, "you could get at least 100 times as much for this picture." "Well," explained the woman, "my husband died two weeks ago and stipulated in his will that the picture was to be sold and the money given to his secretary. And I," she added triumphantly, "am the executrix of his will!"

A Is for Aunt: Mary Lou's aunt asked her to stop at her office and pick up her pay envelope. A short time later, a wild-eyed Mary Lou dashed up to a policeman and wailed, "Oh, Sergeant, I've lost my aunt's pay!" "Never mind the pig Latin," the unperturbed cop replied. "Just tell me where you lost them."

A Is for Australia: Australians have a tendency to turn the "a's" into "i's." An American was in an Australian hospital as a result of an automobile accident. When he regained consciousness he asked the nurse: "Was I brought here to die?" and the nurse said, "No, you were brought here yester-die."

A Is for Automobiles: The best way to stop that noise in your car is to let her drive.

Burns and Allen were driving one night when they ran out of gas. Poor George had to hike ten miles with a heavy can to the nearest garage. "Don't forget to look for a station that gives green stamps," said Gracie.

A woman driver wouldn't have as much trouble squeezing into a parking space if she would imagine it was a girdle or a pair of shoes.

B Is for Beatnik:

"Just draw, Faverly, and stop saying 'I've seen better' each time a girl poses."

B Is for Bachelor: Steve Masters, of the Masters Discount House, parsed the word "bachelor" for me. A bachelor is a guy who wants to have a girl in his arms without having her on his hands.

A bachelor is a man who never makes the same mistake once.

B Is for Bank: A woman went into the bank and noticed there was a new face behind the window. "Has the cashier gone away to take a rest?" she inquired. "No," replied the new man, "he's gone away to avoid it."

B Is for Baseball: Yankee star Mickey Mantle stumbled in the field and aggravated a knee injury he'd had since high school. He was rushed to the hospital and put under observation for several days. One afternoon, between examinations, he sat on the terrace and started chatting with an elderly co-patient, a lady who was quite unfamiliar with the baseball world. "How did you hurt your leg, son?" the woman asked. "Playing ball," Mickey answered. "Oh," snorted the matron, "won't you boys *ever* grow up?"

B Is for Bill: When the waiter brought the bill, the diner complained, "What's this five dollars for?" The waiter answered patiently, "A chopped liver sandwich." The diner screamed, "Who's liver was it—Rockefeller's?"

B Is for Bird: Here's a shaggy bird story. As you know, lovebirds are so devoted that if one dies, legend says, the other dies of a broken heart shortly afterwards. Confronted with such a tragic situation, an ingenious pet owner stuck a mirror inside the cage of the surviving lovebird. The lonesome bird, seeing his image, emitted a joyous chirp, snuggled contentedly against the mirror and lived happily for many years. Then one day a careless clerk upset the cage, dropped it to the marble floor and caused the lovebird to die—of a broken mirror.

B Is for Birthdays: My wife wanted some pearls for her birthday so I gave her an oyster and a rabbit's foot.

There's the story about the fellow who each day walked to work and passed a window where he saw a lady hitting a boy over the head with a loaf of bread. The fellow decided it was none of his business and walked on. He saw this same thing happen every morning for five months—each day, the lady hitting the boy with a loaf of bread. Then one morning he saw the woman toss an entire chocolate cake into the boy's face. Astounded, he peered into the open window and asked why. "Oh," the lady said, "it's his birthday."

B Is for Bopsters: Two bopsters were attending a concert when a fire broke out. All the musicians cleared the stage and the audience began heading for the exits. "Come on, man, let's beat it," said one. "You go ahead, man," replied the pal. "I want to dig this crazy finale."

Two bopsters visited the Swiss Alps. A skier whizzed down the chute, then up into the sky. "We're in luck, man," grooved one bopster, "somebody here sells our brand of cigarettes."

B Is for Borneo: I met a scientist in Borneo who's working on a hair formula. He has no formula for growing more curls but they have a way of shrinking your head to fit the hair you've got.

B Is for Boss: Two men were discussing their employers. "My boss," said one, "is a no-good cheapskate. He should only drop dead." "My boss," smiled the second, "is different. You just can't help liking him 'cause if you don't he fires you."

The new maid was the slowest thing on two feet. It took her at least three times as long as anyone else to do something. One day, the boss of the house reached her boiling point. "You're worse than a snail," she screamed. "Tell me, Alice, is there anything you can do fast?" Alice thought for a moment and then replied, "Get tired."

B Is for Budget: Asked the meaning of the word "budget," one little boy replied, "It's a family quarrel."

B Is for Butcher: A woman walked into a butcher shop and told the owner, "That chicken I bought from you yesterday had no wishbone." The butcher answered, "Madam, our chickens are so contented that they have nothing to wish for."

C Is for Charge Account:

C Is for Cabby: This is a Hy Gardner classic: It all started in front of the Waldorf-Astoria. A mink-befurred, lorgnette-dangling dowager, with trunks and suitcases stacked up like planes over Idlewild, was helped into a cab while a second taxi took care of her excess. "Mrs. Whittlestick," the uniformed doorman said, "wishes to be driven to Pier 8. She's sailing on the S.S. *United States.*" The hackie nodded, dropped the flag and beckoned with his little finger to have the baggage car follow.

In no longer than it takes to read a union contract, the cabs arrived at the pier, the baggage was checked into state-rooms A through X, and the passenger spoke to the cabby. "If you're single and want to double your income, I'd like to offer you a proposition to see the world through your own windshield. I simple loathe hailing strange cabs in strange places. How would you like to drive me around Europe, all expenses paid?"

The hackie's mouth opened, but no words came out. Finally he nodded. In a few minutes arrangements were made to have the cab hoisted into the hold of the ship, where it remained till the ship berthed in Le Havre. From there they drove to Paris, then Nice, then Monte Carlo, then back to Paris for the channel crossing to England, then to Rome, Berlin and through the Scandinavian countries. Like the cab's two occupants, the meter never stopped running. Eventually, the party retraced its tire treads, the *United States* docked again at the point of origination, Pier 8. The cab was hoisted out of the hold and plunked on terra firma.

"Well, my good man," the fatigued dowager sighed, paying the $12,457 clicked on the clock, "we're on native soil again, thank goodness. Now will you please drive me home?" "Where is home, ma'am?" the hackie smiled. "It's near Prospect Park, in Brooklyn," his benefactor replied. "Brooklyn!" the hackie snorted, slamming the door. "Are you nuts? You'll have to take another cab. Every time I go to Brooklyn I have to come back to Manhattan empty!"

C Is for Calcutta:

> There was a guy in Calcutta
> Talked with a cute little stutter
> He screwed up his face
> When he tried to say grace
> And blew his false teeth in the butter.

C Is for Canada: Up in Canada they have an organization called The Northwest Mounted. They have the reputation of always getting their man. We got the same thing here in this country, we call it "The Draft" (or Selective Service).

It gets so cold in the northern Canadian Woods, the women wear mink girdles.

C Is for Cannibal: Let's tell about this cannibal. He was dressed up in European fashion, sent to college and grew to maturity in the ways of civilization. Then came his first trip on a luxury liner. Now, the former cannibal went for his first sitting in the first-class dining saloon. In most decorous fashion, the steward asked him: "Would you like to see the menu?" "No," sez he, "I'd like to see the passenger list."

C Is for Casablanca: My uncle heard of the Adventures in Casablanca but when he goes there it will become just an Adventure in Casablanca . . . he's too old to have more than one.

C Is for Caterpillar: Two caterpillars were munching away on a cabbage leaf. A butterfly fluttered in the air above them. One caterpillar noticed the butterfly and said to the other, "You'll never get me up in one of them things."

C Is for Cheapskate: He's so cheap that the only time he'll pick up a check is when its made out to him.

C Is for China: An American standing at a bar in Hong Kong got into a conversation with the Chinaman standing next to him. When the American asked what he did, the Chinaman said, "Oh, I was a Chinese airman, I fight in Korea." The American asked him his name and he said, "My name is Chow Mein, I was a Kamikaze flier." The American said, "Who are you kidding, Chow Mein? I was a flier, too, and I happen to know if you were a Kamikaze flier you wouldn't be here right now. That was a suicide squad!" The Chinaman grinned and said, "Oh, me Chicken Chow Mein."

A tourist in China watched as three prominent Chinese were being buried. As the first casket was lowered, several

Chinese women came forward, placing chickens, rice, bread and wine on the coffin. "What's that for?" asked the visitor. "That is our custom," answered one of the mourners, "so that the body of the dead man will not go hungry." The same procedure was followed when the second casket was lowered. When the third was lowered only a single cup of rice was placed on it. "Say," muttered the stranger, "how come they put such a little bit of food on that coffin?" The Chinaman shrugged. "That was Sing Lee. He was on a diet."

When a Jewish kid gets Bar-Mitzvahed in China, he says, "Today I am a man-darin."

In China it's custom for a man never to take a girl out until he marries her. In this country he never takes her out afterwards.

C Is for Chorus Girl: A chorus girl may not understand politics, but she sure can put a motion before the house.

C Is for Cold: It was so cold in Florida, they were selling frozen orange juice right off the trees.

It was so cold that the farmers had to milk their cows with ice picks.

C Is for College: It took her four years to get a sheepskin—and one day to get a mink.

C Is for Convict: As he was strapping the convict in the electric chair, the warden asked, "Have you any final wish?" "Yes," answered the book-of-etiquette victim with a sly glance at the prison matron, "allow me to give my seat to a lady."

Two convicts telling how they got in jail. One said: "I had the car so long that I completely forgot I had stolen it when I reported it stolen."

C Is for Counterfeiter: Number 32146, whom we'll call Blinky for short, was only recently taken from the mental ward of a prison and assigned a regular cell. It all dates back to the reason for his incarceration. Blinky was known as the Grandpa Moses of counterfeiters. He was so meticulous copying a bill it took the eagle eye of a trained professional to detect his funny money from the real McCoy. For many months Blinky worked on what he thought was a foolproof set of engravings for a $10 bill. His chore completed, he wrinkled his work of art, compared it with the original through a powerful magnifying glass and decided to test-pass it before going into volume production. Within two hours Blinky was arrested. "I defy you," he raged at the Treasury agent, placing both the original and the spurious bill side by side, "to tell me the difference between these two ten-spots." "There is no difference, Blinky," the T-man agreed, "and that's the trouble. Seems you only made one mistake. You copied your counterfeit from a counterfeit!"

This counterfeiter was going out of the business. So, in a last big fling, he made a $15 bill. He went into a candy store, bought a couple of 50-cent stogies and handed over the bill. The clerk looked at it for a moment and went into the back of his establishment, came out and gave him two $7 bills in change.

C Is for Creditors: I met a fellow in Hawaii who told me he went there for respiratory trouble. He said back home his creditors wouldn't let him breathe easy.

C Is for Cuba: They're always talking about those beards the Castro followers are wearing. What's the big idea? I got an uncle, and a beard like that on him is merely a five-o'clock shadow.

D Is for Dance: A neighbor of mine and his wife took up mamboing very seriously, but I saw them the other night on the dance floor. While the wife was doing the mambo—he was doing the samba. I asked him how come and he said he was trying to quit by tapering off. . . .

D Is for Divorce:

"They decided to settle it out of court."

D Is for Dentist: A Tulsa, Oklahoma oilman gushed into his dentist for an examination. The dentist dove into the Oillionaire's mouth and said, "Perfect, man, perfect! You don't need a thing." "Well, drill anyway, Doc," the patient drawled, "I feel lucky this morning."

The dentist examined the nervous lady and finally said, "It looks like I'll have to pull your tooth." The woman squealed, "I'd rather have a baby." The doctor countered, "Make up your mind, lady, before I adjust the chair."

D Is for Diet: Americans have more food to eat than people of any other nation on earth and more diets to keep us from eating it.

I just quit my onion diet. I lost ten pounds but twelve friends.

This is the prayer of a small girl: "Please, Lord, can't you put the vitamins in pie and cake instead of cod-liver oil and spinach?"

D Is for Diners' Club: A disgruntled would-be joiner wrote a long and sordid letter to the Diners' Club claiming he couldn't understand why he was not acceptable. At the end he explained that he would like to get an answer and please address it to the hotel on the letterhead. "This hotel," he said, "is one of my better creditors."

The funniest story going around Madrid, Spain, at the moment, happened the other evening at one of the best night clubs there. It seems that a certain newspaperman was attracted to a certain dancer at this club and asked if he might take her to another cabaret. The headwaiter said that such a thing could be arranged if the newspaperman was willing to pay for her time. At the moment the scribe didn't have sufficient pesetas and asked if he could cash a traveler's check. The headwaiter said no, but if the chap had a Diners' Club card he would charge off the date as dessert. And the deal was actually made!

D Is for Doctor: The doctor rushed out of his study and instructed his wife, "Get me my bag at once!" "What's the matter?" she asked. "Some fellow just phoned and said he couldn't live without me." The wife thought a few seconds, then, "Just a moment," she said gently, "I think that call was for me."

Back home in East Texas, Old Man Jones confessed his troubles to the local doctor. "It's sort of ticklish to talk about, Doc," he apologized. "But I need some vitamins or something on account of when it comes to making love, I ain't got as much pep as I used to have." "Well, that's natural," the Doc consoled, "how old are you?" "Well, let's see. I'm a year older'n my wife and she's eighty-one. Guess I'm about eighty-two years of age." "And when did you first notice this lack of pep on your part?" "Well, the first time was last night. That wasn't so bad, but be-dogged if we didn't notice it again this morning."

The woman ear and throat specialist was all in a tizzy. Seems she wanted to paint the throat of a very chic patient—the trouble was she couldn't decide on a color!

DOCTOR: The check you gave me came back.
PATIENT: So did my arthritis.

D Is for Double Talk: Al Kelly, the world's greatest double-talk artist, had a fight with his wife and she finally told him he must be smarter than Einstein. "Twelve people understand Einstein," she said, "but you—you—nobody understands."

D Is for Drink: Now that Alaska and Hawaii are States, the most popular American drink will probably be pineapple juice with ice in it.

D Is for Drinker: A heavy drinker was regaling his friends with his early life and the hard times he had. "Things were so bad," he recalled, "that sometimes I had to live for days on nothing but food and water."

A husband returned home late one night in a rather inebriated state and handed the wife his pay envelope. She opened it, looked inside and shouted, "This is only half your salary. Where's the rest of it?" "I bought something for the house," he explained. "Oh, how nice," smiled the spouse. "What'd you buy?" To which her husband replied, "A round of drinks."

Lovable clown Joe E. Lewis has been warned many times about his drinking. "Don't worry about a thing," is Joe's answer, "I'm responsible for a new surgical technique. After my last operation, instead of stitches they used corks."

D Is for Drunk: There are plenty of good cures for hangovers. One is to stay hungover. Eddie Condon's recipe starts like this: *Take the juice of one quart of whisky . . .*

As the Poet Laureate of the drunks once said, "Each man kills the thing he loves." And with that, he opened up a fifth of rye.

A boozer weaved into a bar and ordered a Scotch. After one drink he took his pants off. The bartender wanted to know what was going on or coming off. "I always take my pants off when I drink," hicc'd the man. "It's comfortable. Try it." So the bartender took his pants off and he agreed that it was comfortable. A few of the other drinkers saw and decided to go along. They took their pants off. Pretty soon all the 23 customers in the joint and the bartender were standing around and drinking—just wearing their shorts. A Joe E. Lewis protégé, who had been trying to outdo the master at all the neighborhood bars, staggered in, took a bead on them and muttered, "What are you guys going to do if you get rejected?"

Joe E., by the way, was the boy who went to the store and asked the grocer for a fifth of milk. But now he says he's planning to give up drinking. "I'm beginning to see the handwriting on the floor."

A man was shocked when, inside a bar, he spotted his friend who had been a member of Alcoholics Anonymous for two years. "Sam, how come?" he asked. "It's nothing," came the reply, "I'm just tapering on."

A motorist was speeding down a country road when his car suddenly veered sharply, hit a soft shoulder, rolled over four times and wound up in the middle of a cornfield. A farmer, hoeing nearby, rushed over and saw the driver slowly crawl out. "That was a mighty bad spill you had there," the farmer remarked, "have you been drinking?" "You darn fool," the driver screamed at him, "of course I've been drinking— What do you think I am, a stunt driver?"

E Is for Eating:

E Is for Efficiency Expert: An efficiency expert died and was being carried to his grave by six pallbearers. As they approached their destination the lid popped open and the efficiency expert sat up and shouted, "If you'd put this thing on wheels, you could lay off four men."

A woman was telling her friend about her husband's job. "My husband is an efficiency expert for a large company." "What's an efficiency expert?" her companion asked. "Well, put it this way," the spouse explained; "if we women did it, they'd call it nagging."

E Is for Egypt: This is a shaggy camel story: When the party got to Egypt midway on their world cruise, naturally the first thing they decided to visit was the pyramids. Approaching a drive-it-yourself camel dealer, the tourists inquired how much it would cost to rent a camel. "That depends," the camel man said, "do you want one lump or two?"

E Is for England: There's a university in England so conservative that it refuses to teach liberal arts courses.

A member of the faculty of a London medical college was chosen to be honorary physician to the Queen. Proud of his appointment he wrote a note on the blackboard in his classroom: *Beginning next month,* it said, *I will be honorary physician to Queen Elizabeth.* The next day when the professor returned to his classroom, he found the following line written below his notice: *God Save the Queen.*

A visitor from London, startled at dead of night by a terrifying hoot, asked his host, "What's that?" "It's an owl," he was told. "I know," smiled the Britisher, "but who's 'owling?"

A couple of G.I.'s in Piccadilly were hoisting their third pint of bitters at a neighborhood pub when one nudged the other, saying, "Max, I think that high-classh, tony-lookin' gent hanging onto the barshtool there ish the Archbishop of Canterbury." "You're shtupid drunk," hicc'd the other, "what's the Archbishop of Canterbury gonna be doing here in a creepy bar guzzling beer?" "*I'm* drunk? *I'm* drunk?" yelled the first. "That'sh what I shaid. You're drunk." "Anyway, I say he's the Archbishop." "You're crazy." Two pints of bitters later, Max reeled off his chair and teetered toward the high-class tony-lookin' gent to see if he really was the Archbishop of Canterbury. When he asked the question, the man cursed him, his ancestors, his children, smacked him in the teeth, stepped on him, kicked him, told him to mind his own business and stalked out angrily. "Too bad," said Max, "now we'll never know."

After being injured in a cricket match (which wasn't cricket—it was crooked) the English sportsman went to a doctor who put three stitches in his wound. "That'll be five pounds," the M.D. told him. "Five pounds?" howled the injured one, "for three stitches?" "That's right," smiled the doctor. "Boy," said the patient, "am I happy you're not my tailor."

After spending a year at Oxford, the son of an old English nobleman returned home for his summer vacation. "And now that you've spent a year at the University, what did you find the hardest thing to deal with?" the old man asked. His son answered, "An old deck of cards."

A brilliant but homely English diplomat, sure he would land a position at the British Embassy in Washington, was heartbroken when he was nixed at zero hour. "I say, sir, but why was I turned down?" he asked his superior. "There's no doubt, Chauncey old man, that you're a whizz at foreign affairs," he was told, "but we cahn't possibly send anyone to Washington who doesn't look good before a TV camera."

A snobbish young Britisher who was so Britttttish he could barely talk a-tall visited Washington's home in Mount Vernon. He was promenading through the gardens when he spotted a hedge that looked like one he had back home in Stratfordshire on the Hertfordshire. "Ah, my good chap," he told the caretaker, "you see that hedge? George got that from jolly old England." "I don't doubt it," smiled the gardener. "As you probably know, he got this whole blooming country from England."

An American boasted to an Englishman about the speed of American trains. "In America," he bragged, "our trains are so fast that telegraph poles look like a continuous fence." "Ha," snuffed the Britisher, "that's nothing. I was on such a fast train in England last week that I passed a field of turnips, a field of carrots, one of cabbage and then a pond . . . and we were going so fast that I thought it was broth."

British Guide (showing place of interest): It was in this room that Lord Wellington received his first commission.
American Tourist: How much was it?

A man toddled into a London antique shop and offered for sale a piece of silk he claimed to be part of Sir Walter Raleigh's garment. The proprietor called his assistant, "Oh Newton!" and Newt shuffled forward, affixed his eyeglass, studied the silk and wheezed, "It's Sir Walter's all right, but we have two yards of the same thing in our storeroom." Next day the man returned with a piece of the original Ark, and again the owner called, "Oh Newton!" and again Newt came forward, affixed his eyeglass, examined it and said, "It's from the Ark but we have the rest of it in our storeroom." The following week the same man returned. He told the owner he had one of Nero's eyes and said, "And don't send for Newton. I have the other one in my pocket."

E Is for Enterprise: A high-pressure auto salesman told his customer, "Do you realize that while you're standing here dickering, your car is depreciating?"

E Is for Executive: A good executive is a man who believes in sharing the credit with the man who did the work.

An executive came home one night and slumped unhappily into his favorite chair. Noticing his state, his wife asked what was wrong. "Well," he moaned, "you know those aptitude tests I'm giving over at the office? I took one today and it sure is a good thing I own the company."

E Is for Exercise: A trim-looking octogenarian was asked how he maintained his slim figure. "I get my exercise," he boasted, "acting as a pallbearer for all my friends who exercise."

E Is for Explanation: Myron Cohen says this drunk was walking along Fifth Avenue at 4 A.M. in a state of panic. A cop approached him and growled, "Do you have an explanation?" The poor soul answered, "If I would have an explanation, I would be home with my wife."

F Is for Fat:

Girl right: *"Who's the dame Ed is talking to?"*
Girl left: *"Oh! She's a big game hunter. Last year she downed an elephant in Africa."*
Girl right: *"You mean! Whole?"*

F Is for Fight: I had a terrible fight with my wife. I said, "You know, you're going to drive me to my grave." In two minutes she had the car in front of the house.

F Is for Fishermen: Two fishermen were trying to convince some friends of their luck. "I went fishing the other day," lied one, "and caught one of these big fish—let me see, what is it you call them?" he asked, turning to his fibbing partner. "Oh yes, you mean—whale," assisted the second fisherman. "No, not that," protested the first, "that couldn't have been it; I was using whale for bait!" "And the fish we finally caught," said the second fisherman, "was too small to bother with, so we got a couple of men to help us throw it back into the water."

F Is for Florist: What do you send to a sick florist?

F Is for France: An American and French bride were discussing love. "A Frenchman is very subtle when it comes to love," the French girl explained. "He begins by kissing the finger tips, then he kisses the shoulder, then the back of the neck . . ." "Boy," the little American bride interrupted, "by that time an American husband is back from his honeymoon!"

In France, the postman isn't the only poor working person who has to walk the streets to pick up the male.

Modern French Westerns are so adult that instead of having a bartender, the local saloon has a maître d'.

The proud old Frenchman put on the uniform and all the medals he had worn during his glory days in the First World War. He looked into the mirror and remembered how it had been. He noticed his five-year-old grandson staring at the medals. "What's the matter, lad?" he asked. "Oh nothing, Grandpa, but I was wondering why you're wearing your money outside your coat?"

During the German occupation of France a peasant who worked for the underground was captured. Now and then he received a letter from his wife, who complained she was having a difficult time with their farm. She had plenty of seed potatoes but she couldn't plow the fields herself. He wrote back, *It is all for the best, ma chère. Leave the fields unplowed. That's where the guns are.* Four days later two truckloads of Gestapo men descended on the farm and dug up all the acreage. Frantically the wife wrote to her husband telling him what had happened and asked him what to do. He wrote back a brief note. *Now plant the potatoes.*

A Brooklynite, touring Gay Paree, stopped a Frenchman and asked, "Where's the place that most of the Americans stay?" The Frenchman replied, "The first ten rows of the Folies Bergère."

My friend laughed when I spoke to the waiter in French but the laugh was on him. I told the waiter to give him the check.

A French husband raced into a psychiatrist's office and shouted, "Doc, you've got to help me. My wife thinks she's Brigitte Bardot." The headshrinker thought for a moment and then told the fellow, "If you bring her in for treatments, I'm sure I can help her." "That's wonderful, Doc," the man smiled, "but make sure your office is heated because my wife always goes around in the nude and I wouldn't want her to catch a cold."

The scene is a Paris street corner. A shady-looking character approaches a New York tourist and after glancing in all directions to see that he's safe, nudges the tourist and the following gab follows: *"Americain?"* ... "Yeah." ... "Tourist?" ... "Yeah." ... "Want Whoopie?" ... "Naaah." ... "Post cards?" ... "Naaah." ... "Strip-tease night club?" ... "Naaah." ... "Strip tease without night club?" ... "Naaah." ... "Model posing for artist?" ... "Naaah." ... "Artist posing for model?" ... "Naaah." ... "Kosher delicatessen?" ... "Ah ha, now you're talking."

Two Parisians, François and Louis, got into an argument about a lady, and before you knew it one word led to another and thousands more followed, so they finally agreed to settle the matter by a pistol duel in the park. At 7 on the appointed morning, François was on hand with his pistol and his second and his physician, but no Louis. A few minutes later a messenger arrived with a note from Louis which read: *Dear François, if I happen to be late, don't wait for me, go ahead and shoot.*

From France comes the story of twin brothers in a historic French family. One was raised to become a soldier, the other a priest. But, as brothers sometimes do, they disliked each other intensely and had been away from each other for many many years. One day they finally came face to face in the Eastern Station of Paris. By now the older brother had become a marshal of France and the younger brother a cardinal. As the Prince of the Church saw his brother on the platform, a mischievous smile appeared on his lips and walking over to the soldier he said, "Pardon me, Station Master, but when is the next train for Metz?" The Marshal blinked for a moment, then saluted smartly and said, "Sorry, I really don't know, madame."

Things must be getting tough in France. I just got a post card from Paris and there was writing on it.

In France, the men like to stay out until the "Oui" hours of the morning.

F Is for Funerals: A group of townspeople were seated in a local barbershop attempting to eulogize a citizen who had just died. For years the fellow had been the most hated man in town and no one could think of anything good to say about him. Eventually, after more than an hour of silence, the barber spoke up. "You know," he said, "I must admit he wasn't a hard man to shave."

A New York newspaper, in an article on air-raid procedures, stated, *Funeral coaches also must park, but the occupants may remain in them.*

A New Hampshire farmer had been urged to attend the funeral of his neighbor's third wife. "But I'm not going," he announced to his own spouse. "Goodness sakes, why not?" she asked. "Well, Mary, I'm beginnin' to feel kind of awkward about goin' so often without anything of the sort to ask him back to."

F Is for Fur Coat: Right before I went on the air one night, I was handed this note: *Will the man who found a fur coat here in the studio last week please return the blonde that was in it.*

F Is for Furrier: It seems there's a New York furrier who has been trying to get a longer-lasting, cheaper fur by mating a mink with a chimpanzee, but it doesn't work . . . the sleeves are too long.

G Is for Gambling: I wouldn't say the roulette wheel was crooked, but how come the table says TILT?

One gambling hotel in Las Vegas will send a table and dealer to your room. "That's what we call room service here," the manager bragged.

It's still tougher to make a six with two threes than a Gabor with two Zsas.

Nevada is famous for its gambling. This is one place where money isn't everything—if you stay there long enough, it's nothing.

G Is for Germany: Two Germans were talking. One said, "Do you know, if Hitler had lived he would have been seventy?" And the other German said, "Too bad, too bad." The first one asked, "What d'ya mean, too bad? That he's dead?" And the second German said, "Oh, no, that he was born!"

A German and Russian were on a river in Germany. The German was fishing on the American side and was catching fish right and left, one after the other, but the Russian on the Russian Zone side wasn't having any luck at all. He yelled to the German, "How do you manage to catch so many fish?" and the answer came back, "Over here the fish aren't afraid to open their mouths."

G Is for Gratitude:

"She likes making our job as pleasant as possible—"

They tell the story in Berlin about an argument between an American officer and a Russian officer over what constituted democracy and in which country the real democracy was truly practiced. The American said, "Why, back home a fellow living out in the midwestern part of the country can hop a train, be in Washington in a couple of days, walk down Pennsylvania Avenue, make arrangements to get into the White House and walk into the President's office and say, 'Mr. President Eisenhower, you're a stupid man.' He can do that and he wouldn't even be arrested." The Russian officer said, "That's exactly the kind of democracy we have in

Russia. A peasant from any small village could start out for Stalingrad, get there in a couple of months—maybe—spend another few months getting to Moscow, go to the Kremlin, walk in, knock on Khrushchev's door and say, 'Comrade Khrushchev, President Eisenhower is a stupid man'—and believe it or not, the peasant would not even be arrested."

Too bad Hitler isn't alive today—just look at all those houses in Germany that need painting.

G Is for Girl: A girl who was taking a fishing trip off the coast of Florida wired her friend back home: THE BIGGEST FISH WAS CAUGHT BY A GIRL FROM OHIO. HE'S FROM TEXAS AND HAS 23 OIL WELLS.

I've been interested in girls ever since I was fourteen. I got a job as part-time skirt-blower at Coney Island. It really opened my eyes.

G Is for Girlfriend: My girlfriend is very rich. She winters in Miami, summers in Maine and springs at every man she sees.

I have been married thirty years and I'm still in love with the same woman. If my wife ever finds out, she'll kill me.

G Is for Golf: A minister's assistant was watching while a member of the congregation was beating the minister at golf. He walked over to the fellow and whispered in his ear, "Remember the cloth, sir." "Cloth?" answered the congregant. "This is golf, not billiards."

G Is for Greece: An American tourist was gazing down into the crater of a famous Greek volcano. Finally he commented, "It looks like Hell!" "Oh, you Americans," said his guide, "you've been everywhere."

G Is for Guide: "This, ladies and gentlemen, is the largest waterfall in the Alps. May I ask the ladies to cease from talking for a little while so that we may hear the roar of the waters."

H Is for Homework:

"Well, you said I was fired, and I should take my things."

H Is for Hawaii: In Hawaii they have the same weather all year round. Then how do they start their conversations?

In Hawaii they're certainly farm-minded. They're always rotating their crops.

I followed two gals around for a week in Honolulu, with a lawn mower.

H Is for Henpecked: He's so henpecked that the only time he opens his mouth is to ask his wife where the mop is.

You can always tell a henpecked husband in a brawl. He's the one who holds his wife's coat.

H Is for Heredity: Real Estater Lou Sacher socked me with this fact: Parenthood is hereditary. If your parent didn't have children, chances are you won't have any either.

H Is for High Fidelity: Daffy-nition of high fidelity—a drunk who comes home to his wife every night.

H Is for Home: A healthy home is a happy home—so send your house to the doctor twice a year.

H Is for Honeymoon: The honeymoon is over when the groom stops wearing his toupee around the house.

H Is for Horseplayer: So this horseplayer died last week and a friend called another friend who was in residence at Gulfstream. He told the pal in the South about the funeral arrangements and then admitted he couldn't remember the name of the cemetery. "It doesn't make any difference," he finally decided. "When you get to La Guardia, take a cab and its the third cemetery on the way to Aqueduct."

H Is for Hotel: An upstate hotel received a reservation request for next season from a Brooklynite who wrote: *Please reserve a suitable room where I can put up with my wife.*

Phil Schweidel, the travel agent, heard this one from one of his clients: The man complained to the manager of a small-town hotel about his accommodations. "This is the best we have," said the manager defensively. "This is the royal suite." The man cracked, "The last royalty that slept here must have been King Kong."

I just came back from a hotel so ritzy that when the guests pitch horseshoes, they have to wear a riding habit.

H Is for Hungary: A visitor to Hungary asked one of the natives, "How many people would you estimate are against the Communist regime here?" and the native said, "Six." The visitor said, "Only six? Are you sure, only six?" The native replied, "Yes, six—you, I, he, she, we and they."

H Is for Hunter: Jack Spitzer, the Albany Ford dealer, drove home with this: A few weeks ago I went out on a hunting trip with a friend of mine in the clothing business. We were walking through the woods when all of a sudden a huge bear came out from behind a tree and leaped at me. I screamed, "Help me, is that a bear?" My friend said, "How should I know? Do I deal in furs?"

H Is for Husband: Mr. Kelly believed emphatically that a husband was entitled to a night out alone each week. So every Tuesday night he went out. Well, one Tuesday he went out and didn't return. Exactly seven years later, he returned home on a Tuesday and his wife was so happy to see him that she began to phone all her friends. "What do you think you're doing?" asked Mr. Kelly suspiciously. "Why, arranging a welcome home party for you tonight," answered Mrs. Kelly. "What!" protested her husband. "On my night out?"

H Is for Hypnotism: Hypnotism is getting a man in your power and making him do what you want—that's not hypnotism, that's marriage!

H Is for Hypochondriac: It's easy to spot a hypochondriac. He's the guy who can read his doctor's handwriting.

I Is for Iceland: In Iceland I saw a sign that read BEWARE OF POLAR BEAR, SIGNED FRIENDLY ESKIMO. Then I went farther and I saw another sign that read DISREGARD FIRST NOTICE, SIGNED HUNGRY POLAR BEAR.

Have you heard about the northern Eskimo who said to the southern Eskimo, "Glub glub glub" and the southern Eskimo said, "'Glub glub glub, you-all."

I Is for Iceman: Two icemen were talking. Said the first: "If you lived in Turkey, how many wives would you have?" "About as many as I have now."

I Is for Income Tax: Two friends were reminiscing: "Poor old Sam," sympathized one, "he was ruined by untold wealth." "Yeah," said the other, "he should have told about it on his income tax report."

"What do you do when you get a letter from the income tax people?" "I finish reading it on the train."

I Is for Inebriated:

"I told her not to order a double portion of our special rum cake."

The new tax forms are being printed on Kleenex. That's to keep you comfortable while you pay through the nose.

This letter came to the Income Tax Bureau: *Gentlemen, I have not been able to sleep at night because I cheated on last year's income tax. Enclosed find my check for a thousand dollars. If I find I still can't sleep, I'll send you the balance.*

An angry man ran into the post office and shouted to the postmaster, "For some time I've been pestered with threatening letters. I want something done about it!" "I'm sure we can help," soothed the postmaster. "That's a federal offense. Have you any idea who's sending you these letters?" "I certainly do," barked the fellow. "It's those pesky income tax people."

I Is for India: It seems that two Englishmen boarded a train on a very slow trip through India. Now India is a very uninteresting, flat country, so after traveling for two or three days, a conversation finally got started. The first man said, "British?" and after a while the second one said, "Yes." Nothing more was said for two days when the first man in the same low tone with no animation or interest drawled out, "Foreign service?" ... Another pause and the other answered in the same low draggy drawly voice, "Y-e-s." Two days later, the first one spoke up again and asked, "Stationed in Delhi?" and after a long hesitating pause, in the same drawly tone, "Yes." Several more days passed and another question: "Sexual pervert?" ... Another long pause and the answer was "No." ... Two more days went by and the first Britisher, without raising the tone of his voice, mumbled, "Pity."

I Is for Inflation: Herman Soifer of Brookfield Clothes sold me this one: Americans are getting stronger. Twenty years ago it took two people to carry ten dollars' worth of groceries. Today, my child can do it.

I Is for Insane Asylum: An important official who was visiting an insane asylum made a telephone call but had difficulty in getting his number. Finally, in exasperation, he shouted to the operator, "Look here, girl, do you know who I am?" "No," she replied calmly, "but I know where you are."

I Is for Insurance: A fellow who lives in the city most of the year but summers in Maine was surprised one winter day when he received a call from the caretaker of his summer place. "There's a bad forest fire up here," he was informed, "and it looks like your house might get burned down." "My goodness!" the homeowner exclaimed. "Is there anything I can do?" "Well," the caller replied, "I thought maybe you might want to put more insurance on the house."

A man went into the insurance office to report that his car had been stolen and he would like to get his money. The insurance executive was polite but firm: "Sorry, we do not give you money, we replace the car with a new one." The man answered indignantly, "If that's the way you do business, you can cancel the policy on my wife."

I Is for Ireland: Pat walked into a bar in Dublin, his face beaten to a pulp. "And who did that to you?" asked the bartender. "I had a fight with Mike Shannon." "What?" asked the bartender. "You let a little guy like that beat you up? You ought to be ashamed of yourself, a little good-for-nothing runt like Mike." "Hold on there," said Pat, "don't be talking disrespectfully of the dead."

An Irish woman who had reached the age of 102 was giving an interview about her longevity when one of the reporters asked her if she had ever been bedridden and she said, "Oh yis, many times, me bye . . . and once on a sleigh."

A priest once saw a small boy in an Irish town standing on tiptoe trying to reach a doorbell, so the priest climbed the stairs and rang the bell for the lad, who said, "Thanks, Father, now let's run like hell."

In Ireland, a Dublin matron took her young son Sean to enroll in a new school. She said to the headmaster, "Now I want Sean to have a thoroughly modern and up-to-date education including, of course, Latin." The headmaster said,

"Yes, of course, we'll do all we can, but remember, my dear lady, Latin is a dead language." And she said, "All the better —Sean's going to be an undertaker."

I Is for Israel: Much of Israel's humor reflects the day-to-day affairs and tensions under which the Israelis live. It is not surprising, therefore, that many Israeli jokes have to do with war and violence—and even the youngsters reflect the tensions of this new country. There is the story of the little Israeli boy who came home from school and his mother said to him, "What are you doing home so early?" He answered, "Well, I put some dynamite under the teacher's chair." His mother frantically shouted at him, "What a terrible thing to do!! You go right back to school." His noncommittal answer was, "What school, where's school?"

While the Israelis have made a name for themselves with outstanding feats of bravery, they love to kid themselves. They tell the story about the young Israeli soldier who was sent on reconnaissance to investigate the possibility of crossing a bridge. He came back tattered and bleeding and said, "To the right there are tanks and artillery and infantry in heavy numbers. To the left there are numerous atomic war heads and machine guns. I am sure we can go either to the right or to the left, but I'm afraid we cannot cross the bridge." When asked, "Why not?" he said, "They've got a big black dog at the other end."

Rabbi Charles E. Shulman of the Riverdale Temple tells of visiting Israel and asking a native guide whether there were any golf courses there. "Golf?" shrugged the guide. "In a country as tiny as ours, a good golf drive could become an international incident."

Former Ambassador James G. McDonald tells this one. An Israel philharmonic was playing one of the long-haired avant-garde compositions. Mrs. Ben-Gurion nudged her husband. "See, over there, Ben Zvi is sleeping." "For that you have to wake me?" replied Ben-Gurion.

Israel is the greatest place in the world for people. Especially for millionaires. Why? No millionaire has died there yet.

Someone who recently waited her turn in a grocery queue in Jerusalem passed along this story to the Jerusalem *Post*: A housewife was trying to buy more than one bottle of a popular detergent, of which the grocer had just received a long-awaited supply. She could only have one, she was informed. Whereupon the housewife began a harrowing account of her soap shortage, its effect on the health of her small children, and so on. Finally the grocer softened. "All right," he said, "I'll let you have two if you give me two empty bottles." The happy woman turned to her young daughter and said, "Quick, darling, run home and get two bottles of X from the kitchen." In a few minutes the child returned clutching two full bottles.

An aunt from town visited a *kibbutz* and arrived just in time to see the kindergarten tots playing in the swimming pool—stark naked. "Aren't you ashamed?" she asked her nephew, aged four. He didn't know what she was talking about. A week later, a parcel arrived from the city with a small pair of swimming trunks inside. The little boy put them on and when asked in the pool what the strange garment was for, he replied, "So I can be ashamed."

Not long ago in Tel Aviv a frustrated lover, who had been threatening to kill the girl and her family, jumped off her third-floor balcony when the police approached. By a miracle he escaped injury. Police promptly seized and searched him, finding a pistol and a dollar bill. He was charged with illegal possession of foreign currency.

A rather inexpert father, anxious to make himself useful around the house, undertook to put his small son to bed, a housewife told the Jerusalem *Post* recently. She put supper on the table, trimmed the oil stove and sat down to worry about her next day's chores. Still her husband did not emerge. Then the bedroom door opened softly and the little boy crept out, hushing her, finger to mouth. "Well, Ima (mama)," he said, "the old man is asleep at last."

A public taxi was traveling from Tel Aviv to Haifa. One of its six passengers was an old lady, a new immigrant, who kept asking the driver to tell her when they passed Athlit. She asked him so often that he got nervous, and when they reached Athlit kept right on going before he checked himself. He apologized to the other passengers, turned around and drove back. Turning to the old lady he said, "Here is Athlit; now you can get out." Whereupon she said to him, "Who wants to get out?" The driver, startled, answered, "But you did." "No," answered the old lady, "my daughter told me when I left Tel Aviv that when I pass Athlit, I should take my medicine."

In an effort to keep up with the latest trends, Israel has come out with a gefüllte-tip cigarette.

During the time of the war of liberation, there were not enough guns and ammunition to go around—let alone uniforms. An American volunteer tried to join the Israeli Army. He passed his medical with flying colors, but when he asked for his uniform he was told, "We are a poor country. We cannot afford uniforms." Whereupon the American said he would try the Air Force. He then asked couldn't he at least have a cap or insignia. He again was told no uniforms—this request also could not be fulfilled. So he decided to join the Navy where a uniform is not important on a ship. When he was being interviewed, he was asked if he could swim, whereupon he got up and screeched, "My God, don't you even have ships here?"

One young soldier who was discharged from the Army tried to make his career with the Habimah Theater. After many months he got a substitute part with a single line, "Hark, I hear a cannon." The night of the performance the cannon went off on cue and instead of speaking his line, his surprised reaction was, "What the hell was that!!!"

The brashness of Israeli youth is not confined to the Army, it is also reflected in civilian life. One little boy boarded a crowded bus where he had to stand with no place to hang on. He reached up and held on to the beard of an old man near him. After riding this way for a half-hour the gentleman said to him, "Look, son, you will have to let go." Whereupon the boy in astonishment replied, "What's the matter—are you getting off here?"

One kid came late to school and his excuse was they had a family situation that had to be taken care of. He went on to explain that his father had to take the bull to the cow. When the teacher replied, "Couldn't your father do it himself?" the boy's answer was, "I guess he could, but the bull would do it better."

I Is for Italy: A plane was flying over Italy, then over the Bay of Naples when the pilot turned to his passenger and said, "Pardon me, but have you ever heard of the expression 'See Naples and Die'?" And the passenger said, "Yes, I have, why?" And the pilot said, "Take a good look, the propeller just came off."

Sign in an Italian shop window: DON'T BE MISTAKEN FOR AN AMERICAN TOURIST . . . WEAR ITALIAN-MADE CLOTHES.

The Italian composer Rossini went to see his doctor, and after examining him, the doctor said, "Your trouble stems from wine, women and song." Rossini suggested, "Well, I can get along without the songs, since I compose my own." The doctor said, "Well, which of the other two are you prepared to give up?" And Rossini replied, "That depends entirely on the vintage."

This is a story about a warrior of ancient Rome. He was called off to war and, fearing for the safety of his beautiful young wife, locked her in armor and then summoned his best friend and handed him the key. He said, "My friend, if I do not return in six months, use the key. To you and only you, do I entrust it." Then he galloped off to battle. He hadn't gone but about five miles when he heard hoofbeats in back of him, and looked around; through a cloud of dust his friend rode up and very excitedly cried "Stop! You gave me the wrong key."

Mascagni, the composer, once heard an organ-grinder under his window in Naples playing excerpts from his opera *Cavalleria Rusticana.* The tempo was much too slow and the dragging notes almost drove the composer to distraction. Finally, unable to stand it any longer, he rushed into the street and told the musician, "Here, I am Mascagni. I will show you how to play this music correctly." Thereupon he gave the crank handle of the barrel organ a few rapid turns, thus speeding up the tempo, and said, "There, that is the tempo in which you play." The next day Mascagni heard the organ-grinder playing again and looking out of his window, the organ-grinder had the following sign hanging over his hurdy-gurdy: PUPIL OF MASCAGNI.

J Is for Japan: Japanese Boy's Essay on a Banana: Bananas are remarkable fruit. Him constructed same style as Melican sausage but skin of sausage consumed while it not advisable to eat ripping-off part of banana. Ripping—eh what? Ah so!

An American official in Tokyo had occasion to write to a Japanese businessman there, and thinking to give his letter the flowery Oriental touch that would make for good public relations, closed with these words: *May Heaven preserve you always*—to which the Japanese man replied: *And may Heaven pickle you, too!*

Three American Red Cross girls shared a house in Yokohama and they employed a Jap butler by the name of Togo who, at one time, served on an ocean liner and he clung to the idea that all visitors were to be announced as passengers. The girls took him in hand and briefed him, telling him not to announce the guests as passengers but as callers or visitors

J Is for Junior:

"Why don't you go and play outside?"

or company. Togo assured the girls he knew the proper word and for the girls not to worry. That evening the girls were having a little party and the living room was filled with guests when the doorbell rang, and when Togo saw two male visitors standing there, he turned and rather proudly announced: "Miss Prentiss—two customers for you."

J Is for Judge: "Why don't you settle this case out of court?" the judge asked the two men before him. "That's just what we were doing," replied one fellow, "when the police came and interfered."

The noted jurist was asked how he comes to a decision. "Oh," he said, "I listen to the plaintiff and then I make my decision." "Don't you ever listen to the defendant?" he was asked. "I used to," he said, "but that mixes me up."

An old Southerner who could trace his ancestry back to the time when Lee fought Grant was hauled into court for vagrancy. Brought before the judge, he was asked his name. "It's Colonel Zeth Eaton," he replied. "And what does the 'Colonel' stand for?" the man on the bench asked. "That 'Colonel' is kinda like the 'Honorable' in front of your name," the old man answered. "It doesn't mean a damn thing!"

A Michigan circuit judge tells about a divorce suit he handled recently. "I think you might as well give your husband a divorce," he advised the wife. "What!" shouted the lady. "I have lived with this bum for twenty years, and now I should make him happy?"

A fellow in the New Jersey Court of Chancery recently asked for a divorce on the grounds that his wife didn't love him. The judge asked the husband for proof. "Well, Your Honor," he replied, "only yesterday I was painting our cellar door and when I missed my footing, crashed to the bottom of the steps. My wife rushed to the scene, stared down at my half-conscious form and said, 'While you're down there, Henry, put some coal on the furnace.'"

J Is for Jury: A man had been found dead and the jury was puzzled as to what caused his death. Finally they stated, "It was an act of God under very suspicious circumstances."

J Is for Juvenile Delinquent: He lives in such a ritzy neighborhood that the local juvenile delinquents scribble naughty words on the sidewalk—in French.

K Is for Kids: A three-year-old was struggling with the back button on his new long winter underwear. Finally he gave up, trotted up to his mother and said: "Mommy, open my bathroom door, please."

Did you ever hear the cutie about the lady who sent her four-year-old son to a progressive summer camp? On visiting day she found him all agog about having gone swimming in the camp pool. "But how did you do that?" she asked. "I forgot to pack your bathing trunks." "We went in naked!" the tot explained. "Did the little girls go in naked too?" asked the mother excitedly. "Goodness no, Mother!" the tyke replied. "They wore bathing caps."

"All the neighbors complain about our Freddy," said his mother, "and unfortunately they've got good cause because he's a little rascal!" "Then I'd better buy him a bicycle," said his father. "Why, do you think that will improve his bad behavior?" asked Mother. "Well, no," said Father, "but it will distribute it over a wider area."

A father asked his twelve-year-old son to make a list of the nine greatest men in America. The lad began writing. A few minutes later, the inquisitive parent asked, "Well, how're you getting along?" "I've got nine of them already," the kid smiled, "but I can't make up my mind who to put down for third base."

A little boy asked his mother if he could watch the solar eclipse. "Okay," she replied, "but don't go too close."

K Is for Kommerce:

"Just a lot of worthless junk; but we have to keep in good with them—their air force could be over us in two hours."

A little boy looked at his mother's fur coat and remarked, "How that poor beast must have suffered so that you might have that coat." His mother answered, "Shut up, you shouldn't talk about your father that way."

A little boy asked his father, "Daddy, who gave me my bicycle for Christmas?" "Santa Claus, of course." "Well, Santa was here this morning and said another installment is due."

"Why, I'm ashamed of you, my son," the father screamed at his lazy offspring. "When George Washington was your age, he had become a surveyor and was hard at work." "And when he was your age," shot back the lad, "he was President of the United States."

Two kids came downstairs during a bridge game without a stitch of clothes on. The mother dropped her cards on the table and screamed, "What do you mean by coming down undressed?" "See, smarty," one kid said to the other, "I told you Ma's vanishing cream wouldn't work."

The thoughtful nephew smiled as he asked his rich aunt, "Did you like the chocolates I sent you?" "To tell the truth," she replied, "they haven't come back from the chemist's yet."

Two kids were discussing a young woman who was in the family way. "She ate too much yeast," the first one said loud enough for her to hear him. Annoyed, she barked at him, "Sonny, if your mother had eaten a little more yeast before you were born, you'd be better bred."

The little bud asked Mamma Rose, "Mother, where did I come from?" And Mamma Rose answered, "The stalk brought you."

A little rich boy was picked on by a big rich boy. Said the little rich boy in a fit of pique, "Well anyway, my analyst can lick **your** analyst."

L Is for Loneliness:

"MOTHER!!"

L Is for Landlords: "Was your landlord put out when you asked him to trust you for another month?" "No indeed, I was."

"The landlady was over to the house and she gave Father three days to pay the rent." "What did he do?" "He took Fourth of July, Easter and Christmas."

L Is for Las Vegas: A gambler just back from Las Vegas told his friend he'd undergone Las Vegas surgery. "I had my wallet removed painlessly."

L Is for Laundry: The only trouble with some of these laundries is that they don't leave enough shirt on the cuffs.

"Here, look what you did." "I can't see anything wrong with that lace." "Lace? That was a sheet!"

"Our new minister is so wonderful. He brings things home to you that you never saw before." "I have a laundryman who does the same thing."

"Your laundry is back." "Oh, thanks." "Yeah, they refused it."

L Is for Lawyer: A lawyer was questioning a witness in a murder case. "Did you say that she shot him at close range?" "Yes." "Were there any powder marks on him?" "Sure," came the reply. "That's why she shot him."

The story is told of the lawyer's wife who was complaining about the way their home was furnished. "We need chairs, a dining room set and a new lamp." "Listen," her spouse told her, "one of my clients is suing her husband for divorce. He has a lot of money and as soon as I finish breaking up their home, we'll fix ours."

A lawyer is a fellow who is willing to go out and spend your last cent to prove he's right.

Tombstone: Here lies a lawyer and an honest man. And who'd ever think there'd be room for two men in that one little grave?

L Is for Lazy: His feet have been known to fall asleep while running after a streetcar.

Father says, "Son, go out and see if it's raining" and the son is so lazy he answers, "Oh, Paw, call in the dog and see if he's wet."

Uncle Ed, on relief and employed on a Vermont highway project, complained to the foreman that he wanted a shovel. The foreman told him not to worry about having a shovel, that he'd get paid anyway. "But I want a shovel," insisted Uncle Ed. "Everbody but me's got sunthin' to lean on."

Nathan's wife tells of his discomfiture the time the sheriff's funeral passed their gate. "It was a grand sight," she said. "Nathan was restin' in the hammick when it went by. I come out and told him who all was in the carriages and autymobiles, and his kinfolk wavin' to him. Nathan was kinda peeved. 'Just my luck,' he said, 't'be facin' th' other way.'"

There's the story about the lazy playboy who had so little vitality he stood with the cocktail shaker in his hands waiting for an earthquake.

Has the seven years' itch and is already nine months behind in the scratching.

We've heard of a man who was too lazy to walk in his sleep—he hitchhiked.

The laziest guy in the world handed in an exam paper in which he said the following: *Please see Pete's paper for my answers.*

Two characters were off on a binge. "I'm going to leave this job soon and I want you to come with me," said one of the boys after his eighth drink. "I know a place in Australia where there's a lot of gold just lying around waiting for someone to pick it up." "I knew there was a catch in it," replied the friend. "What's the catch?" "You've got to bend over."

L Is for Lies: "Have you seen one of those instruments to detect falsehoods?" "Seen one? I married one."

"Can you tell by your husband's face if he's lying?" asked one wife of another. And the other snorted, "Yes, if his lips are moving, he is."

"That man is going around telling lies about you." "I don't mind—but I'll break his head if he begins telling the truth."

He tells more lies than a girdle.

L Is for Liquor: Whisky has killed more men than bullets. Maybe so, but wouldn't you rather be filled with whisky than with bullets?

A Westerner entered a saloon with his wife and a three-year-old boy. He ordered two straight whiskies. "Hey, Pa," the kid asked, "ain't Mother drinking?"

L Is for Love: Business is like making love—when it's good it's very good and when it's bad, it ain't bad.

If all the world loves a lover, how come they have cops in Central Park?

He showed her a lot of love and affection. He took her to a drive-in movie and let her peek into the other cars.

An historian was telling his friend that there are no such things as modern and old-fashioned lovers. "Actually," he said, "the art of courting hasn't changed in more than two thousand years. Then, too, Greek maidens used to sit and listen to a lyre all night."

A couple celebrating their 20th anniversary were seated at the movies watching one of those torrid foreign films. When they got home that night, the wife turned to her spouse and purred, "Why is it that you never make love to me like all those men in the movies?" "Are you crazy?" he roared. "Do you know how much they pay those fellows for doing that?"

He loved the girl so much that he worshiped the very ground her father discovered oil on.

Love is valued highest during the days of courting and the days in court.

Love is the only game that is never postponed on account of darkness.

Love is the wine of life, and marriage is the morning after.

"How's your love affair?" "It's all off." "I thought everything was settled?" "It was. I told her my uncle was a millionaire." "What happened?" "Now she's my aunt."

Hollywoodites will go in for pretty near anything as long as it isn't too much trouble and doesn't call for too much risk. The other day on the set, a couple of young extras were talking to me and told me they were going to get married. I said, "Well, are you sure you love each other?" and the boy says, "Well, not exactly, but it won't cost nothin'—my father's a preacher." So I asked the girl if she was sure she loved the boy and she says, "No, but what have I got to lose—my father is a lawyer."

"I don't know why your father don't like me." "Neither do I. After all, money, brains and looks aren't everything."

Love is just a lot of dame foolishness.

He wants to take her away from it all—and she wants to take it all away from him.

He has a soft spot in his head for her.

This week's motto: It is better to have loved and lost than to have run into the house detective.

If love is blind, maybe that's why you see so many spectacles in the park.

A woman set out to reform her fiancé. She got him to give up smoking, then swearing—drinking—chewing tobacco and gambling, and when she finally finished with him, *he* decided she wasn't good enough for him—so he jilted her.

It's better to have loved and lost—yeah, lots better.

L Is for Loyalty: Some women are very loyal. When they reach an age they like, they stick to it.

L Is for Luck: He had tough luck. He had a check for ten dollars and the only person who could cash it was a fellow to whom he owed nine dollars.

NED: Why do you call Ted the luckiest man you ever knew?
RED: He's got a wife and a cigarette lighter—and they both work.

An engineer friend of mine, when taking his shower, slipped on the soap. Then he tore his shirt while he was putting it on. On the way out of the house he fell down the stairs. He finally got out on his run, and as he was traveling 60 miles per hour he looked ahead, and there he saw another train coming toward him at the same speed on the same track. He turned to the fireman and said, "Joe, have you ever had one of those days when everything went dead wrong?"

M Is for Marriage:

"You've got my personal guarantee, miss—there are no loopholes!"

M Is for Manners: A bird in the hand is bad table manners.

"Is my face clean enough to eat with?" "Yes, but you better use your hands."

She's very proper. She won't even look at things with a naked eye.

So polite that when she threw a cup of hot coffee at him, she took the spoon out first.

He embarrassed us—he drank his soup and six couples got up and danced.

My boyfriend is so polite he always knocks on the oyster shells before he opens them.

M Is for Marriage: My wife will put on most anything for dinner except an apron.

"What did you do before you were married?" The husband answered, "Anything I wanted to."

A multimillionaire was telling how he attained his fortune. "I never hesitate," he said, "to give my wife full credit for her assistance." "And just how much did she help?" he was asked. "Frankly," confessed the wealthy one, "I was curious to see if there was any income she could live beyond."

I finally discovered the perfect way to get rid of dishpan hands—I let my husband do the dishes.

There's nothing like a dish towel for wiping that contented look off a married man's face.

The husband complained, "You promised to love, honor and obey— Right now I'd settle for any one of them."

Married men may not be the best-informed men, but they are the most.

The husband asked his wife angrily, "Another new hat! Where will I get the money to pay for it?" She answered, "Whatever my faults, dear, I'm not inquisitive."

There's buried treasure in this country. If you don't think so, listen to some women talk about their first husbands.

A friend tells us about Sam, a successful dress manufacturer, who had to make a trip to the West Coast on business. Sadie, his loving wife, resented the trip bitterly because it meant celebrating their anniversary alone. Plead as she might, Sam couldn't avoid the trip and left his tearful Sadie behind. Every night he called from the Coast and every conversation ended with pain and sobs. Sam had to do something special to prove his own anguish and great love, so one evening he phoned and said, "Sadie dear, I'm sending you two wonderful presents—a Picasso and a Jaguar." And he did. A few days later, Sam asked Sadie during one of their phone conversations, "Didn't the Picasso and the Jaguar arrive yet?" "Not both, Sam," answered Sadie, "only one of them came." "Good! Wonderful!" Sam exclaimed. "Which one?" "Who knows?" answered Sadie.

M Is for Mean: He's so mean he'd send a get-well card to a hypochondriac.

He is so mean that if he killed himself he'd get the right man.

"Honestly, if I could trade places with Robert Taylor or Clark Gable right this minute, I wouldn't do it." "I know you wouldn't. You never do anything to please me."

He is so mean he tears the month of December off his calendars to fool his children.

He was so mean he put a tack on the seat of the electric chair.

A Russian was being led off to execution by a squad of Bolshevik soldiers on a rainy morning. "What brutes you Bolsheviks are, to march me through the rain like this." "How about us? We have to march back."

Speaking of public enemies, I know a guy who gets up at 4 A.M., leans out the window and whistles to wake up the birds.

M Is for Mexico: A wealthy American, touring through a remote section of Mexico, stopped at a lonely little ranch house to ask directions and was surprised to come face to face with what was obviously a 100 per cent American cowboy. He was seated on a magnificent black stallion with the brand BAR-H burned into his skin. The visitor said, "That's a mighty fine horse you have there. If you could only rub out that brand mark I'd give you $2,000 for him." The cowboy said, "Mister, if I ever could rub out that mark I'd still be living in Amarillo, Texas."

M Is for Miser: A surly old miser became extremely ill and in panic sent for his priest. "If I leave $10,000 to the Church," he asked the man of God, "will my salvation be assured?" "I wouldn't say for certain," replied the clergyman, "but it's well worth trying."

M Is for Money: Morris Uchitel, the shoulder-pad man, stuffed me with: Be sure and save your money—you never know when it may be valuable again someday.

Even if money could buy happiness, think what a luxury tax there would be on it.

United States money not only talks—it has learned to speak every foreign language.

You can't see his hidden charms—his money is in Swiss banks.

A man after buying a ticket to a show walked off without picking up his change. The customer next in line asked the cashier what she did in a case like that. "I rap on the window with a sponge," she replied.

A certain producer brags about the fact that he came to this country without a dime in his pocket—and now he owes more than $50,000.

Money may talk but it seems to be very hard of hearing when you call it.

Your wife says she only asks for pin money? Yes, but the first pin she wanted had 12 diamonds in it.

"Money doesn't bring happiness." "Can you prove it?" "Sure, you take a guy with forty million dollars. He ain't happier than a man with thirty-nine million."

Having a little financial trouble—I'm 2 cents overdue on my library card.

Everything is foolish—even the dollar hasn't the same sense it used to have.

Louis Wolfson, the big of the big businessmen, who knows his money, cashed in on this one: "It's called cold cash because we don't keep it long enough to get it warm.

What is the height of being mercenary? Marry Brigitte Bardot for her money.

If a pickpocket would go through my pockets now, all he would get is exercise.

I've been saving for a rainy day. Well anyway, it was a drizzle. Three days of constant rain and I'd be a bum.

M Is for Motel: Xavier Cugat tells the story about the girl, wearied by a long drive, who stopped into a motel looking for a room. The clerk told her that the last room had just been occupied but that there was a couch there and if the man didn't mind her lying down on the couch, it was all right with him. In desperation, she knocked on the door and said to the man, "Look, you don't know me, I don't know you, we don't know them, they don't know us. Can I please bunk on your couch for a while? I won't bother you." "Sure," he said, and went back to sleep. A little while later, she woke him up and said, "Look, you don't know me, I don't know you, we don't know them, they don't know us, do you mind if I just sleep on top of the bed? I won't bother you." "Okay," he said, and fell asleep again. A short while later, she said, "Look, I don't know you, you don't know me, we don't know them, they don't know us, whaddya say we have a party?" "Look," the man said, "if I don't know you, you don't know me, we don't know them, they don't know us—who the hell we gonna invite to the party?!"

M Is for Mother-in-Law: The shortest distance between two points—is the route a groom takes when driving his mother-in-law home.

The daughter called her mother and cried that she wanted to come home to her house. "How will that punish him?" she asked. *"I'll* come to your house."

"My mother-in-law won't stay in this house another moment unless we get rid of the mice." "Say, where are you going?" "To get rid of the cat."

My mother-in-law is a very good cook. I usually get two of her favorites: "Cold shoulder" and "hot tongue."

"Did I actually hear Tommy say that his mother-in-law has the skin he loves to touch?" "That's right; it's sunburned and he likes to hear her holler when he touches it."

"Hello, Higbee. Are you off on a pleasure trip?" "Yes, I'm taking my mother-in-law home again."

M Is for Musician: Definition of a hipster: A musician who knows where the melody is buried.

N Is for Names: Then there's the story about the fellow who excitedly approaches a man walking innocently down a street, slaps him enthusiastically on the back, and shouts, "Abe Minkofsky! Am I glad to see you! But tell me, Abe, what in the world happened to you? Last time I saw you, you were short and fat; all of sudden you're tall and thin. Last time you—" The bewildered man finally was able to interrupt long enough to say, "Look, mister, my name is not Abe Minkofsky." "Ah," boomed the undaunted greeter, "changed your name too, eh?"

N Is for Newlyweds: The newly married pair were stopping in a hotel. The bride left the groom in their room while she went out on a brief shopping expedition. She returned in due time and passed along the hotel corridor to the door, on which she tapped daintily. "I'm back, honey, let me in," she murmured with wishful tenderness. But there was no answer vouchsafed to her plea. She knocked a little more firmly and raised her voice somewhat to call again: "Honey, honey, it's Susie! Let me in!" Thereupon a very cold masculine voice sounded through the door: "Madam, this is not a beehive; it's a bathroom!"

N Is for Neighbors:

"The story you are about to hear is true—only the names have been changed to protect the innocent."

The bride was very much disconcerted at seeing twin beds in their bridal suite. "What's the matter, dearest?" asked the attentive bridegroom. "Why, I certainly thought that we were going to get a room all to ourselves."

N Is for Newspapers: Letter to subscription department, *The New York Times: My son has been reading* THE TIMES *since his confinement to a mental institution. Now that he is cured, I wish to cancel his subscription.*

Vital statistics note in a small-town newspaper: *Due to the shortage of paper a number of births will be postponed until next week.*

N Is for Norway: A Norwegian, during the last war, was talking to the village quisling and asked him what he was going to do when the Allies won the war. The quisling said, "Oh, I'll just put my hat on and leave." The Loyalist said, "Yah, but what are you going to put your hat *on?*"

N Is for Nudist Colony: You can always spot a Peeping Tom at a nudist colony. He's the guy sneaking looks at the girls passing by outside.

It's easy to spot the psychiatrist in a nudist colony. He's the guy who's listening instead of looking.

N Is for Nurse: The Head Nurse was showing the pretty young graduate from nursing school the hospital. As they were walking, the Head Nurse stopped in front of a door of the Men's Convalescent Section. "This is a really dangerous ward," she remarked; "these patients are almost well."

The conceited young man had been in the hospital for some time and had been extremely well looked after by the pretty young nurse. "Nurse," said the patient one morning, "I'm in love with you. I don't want to get well." "Don't worry," replied the nurse cheerfully, "you won't. The doctor's in love with me too, and he saw you kissing me this morning."

The nurse was nicknamed "Appendix" because all the doctors wanted to take her out.

N Is for Nut: A nut hopped into a psychiatrist's office and kept snapping his fingers and growling in low, rumbling tones. "Calm down," said the doctor, "what are you doing that for?" "It keeps away the elephants," was the nut's reply. "There aren't any elephants around here." "See?" said the nut happily, "it works."

O Is for Oops:

"What do you mean you thought he was just clowning around?"

O Is for Office: A young miss just out of business school was filling out an application form (her own form was already filled out) in one of New York's larger advertising agencies. She went through it fine, but when she came to the heading called "Sex," she hesitated. Finally, she decided to answer. *Once in a while,* she wrote.

O Is for Old Age: "My grandfather is ninety-five years old and every day he goes horseback riding—except during the month of July." "Why not during July?" "'Cause that's when the man who puts him on is on his vacation."

He's been smoking since he was fourteen. Now at ninety he's giving it up. He doesn't want to get the habit.

An eighty-five-year-old man was complaining to his friend. "My stenographer is suing me for breach of promise." His friend answered, "At eighty-five, what could you promise her?"

He's so old he gets winded playing chess.

O Is for Old Lady: A recent story concerns the old lady who tottered into a lawyer's office and asked for help in arranging a divorce. "A divorce?" asked the unbelieving lawyer. "Tell me, Grandma, how old are you? "I'm eighty-four," answered the old lady. "Eighty-four! And how old is your husband?" "My husband is eighty-seven." "My, my," myed the lawyer, "and how long have you been married?" "Next September will be sixty-two years." "Married sixty-two years! Why should you want a divorce now?" "Because," Grandma answered calmly, "enough is enough."

O Is for Old Maid: The old maid was asked which she liked most in a man, brains, money or appearance, and she answered, "Appearance—and the sooner the better."

The old maid found a thief under her bed. She held a gun on him and called the police. "Please send a cop over—in the morning."

An old maid is a girl whose father never owned a shotgun.

An old maid was attending a wrestling match when one of the wrestlers was thrown in her lap. She refused to give him up and kept yelling, "Finder's keepers!"

Did you hear about the mean ventriloquist who went around throwing his voice under the bed of all old maids?

O Is for Opportunity: A gent called at the box office of a hit show to purchase a seat. "Not a ticket in the house—you can't buy one for love or money," came the turndown. But this was a persistent customer: "You mean to tell me that if Mayor Wagner wanted to see this show tonight, you couldn't manage to scrape up a ticket for him?" "Yes," came the admission, "if Mayor Wagner needed a ticket, we'd have one for him." "Well," shot back the insistent one, "I got news for you—Mayor Wagner isn't coming and I'd like to have his seat."

You know why I'm a failure? The one time and the *only* time Opportunity ever knocked on my door, I didn't answer. I thought it was the House Detective!

Opportunity knocks but last night a knock spoiled my opportunity.

O Is for Optimists: An optimist is a man who goes to the window in the morning and says, "Good morning, God." A pessimist goes to the window and says, "My God, it's morning!"

Harry Weisbaum, of Beau Brummel Ties, got me in knots with this gag: An optimist is a guy who thinks his wife quit cigarettes because when he came home he found cigar butts all over the house.

An optimist is a guy who falls out of a 20-story building and as he passes every story, he says, "Well, *so far* I'm all right!"

O Is for Orators: If you want to know what an orator is, I'll explain: If you meet a man and ask him how much is 2 and 2 and he says it's 4—he's not an orator. But if you ask another man the same question and he says, "When in the course of human events it becomes necessary to take the second numeral and superimpose it upon the figure two, then I say unto you and I say it without fear of successful contradiction, that the consequential result amounts to four"—Brother, that's an orator!

An orator complained, "When I talk, nobody listens. When money talks—everybody listens."

O Is for Organization: Mr. Cohen belonged to an organization with many social benefits. Each person in the club was asked to buy a plot at a reduced rate—sort of a group plan so they could have a place to live when they died. When the organization found that it wasn't paying off too well, they asked the president to talk to the delinquent members. Cohen was first to be called. "You bought a plot twenty-five years ago," the president began, "and you haven't paid for it yet." The member looked askance. "I didn't use it," he answered. "Who stopped you?" was the topper.

P Is for Parables: The current tension between Russia and the West, and the constant flow of double talk oozing from the mouth of Nikita Khrushchev, recalls a parable Warren Austin related when he was America's first delegate to the United Nations. It concerned a New England farmer who, when asked by his neighbor to lend him an ax, refused, saying: "I'm sorry, but I've got to shave." "How could you possibly offer such a ridiculous excuse?" his wife asked. "It was easy," the farmer shrugged. "When you don't want to do something, one excuse is as good as another."

P Is for Party: This fellow crashed the party. He was there about ten minutes when a dignified gentleman walked over to him and said, "Who are you?" The crasher beamed. "I'm with the groom." "I've got news for you, kid," said the gentleman, "this is a wake—out!"

P Is for Pessimist: Must tell you about the man who was looking so glum and despondent that a friend asked, "Morris, what's eating you? You look like last month's balance sheet." "What's eating me, he asks! Remember two weeks ago, my Tante Razel died and left me $50,000?" "Yeah, I remember, so what's so awful?" "What's so awful, he asks! Remember last week my Uncle Chaim died and left me $75,000?" "I remember that too, but what's bad about that?" "What's bad about it? . . . This week nothing!"

P Is for Party:

"Oh, don't worry—they won't leave—I told them Brigitte Bardot was coming."

P Is for Picnic: This is about the family that went picnicking on a Sunday afternoon. They found a lovely green spot in the country, spread out the tablecloth and covered it with sandwiches, hard-boiled eggs, etc. Impressed by the beauty of the place, they were puzzled by the flags with numbers they saw at various points in the distance. Midway through their picnic, a gentleman strode angrily toward them. "Just what do you think you are doing?" he exploded. "Don't you realize you are sitting on the fifteenth green of the most exclusive golf club in the country?" Papa swallowed his hard-boiled egg and sarcastically answered, "So, this is the way to get new members?"

P Is for Pills: Have you heard about the lad who complained of chronic headaches and was told by his doctor he had a brand-new simply wonderful cure. An atomic pill. "It's really powerful. You take one now," urged the medico, "and call me back in about an hour. Let me know how it worked." An hour later the patient phoned. "Doc," he moaned, "come over right away and pick me up." "Where are you?" asked the doctor. Came the answer: "On 5th Avenue and 50th Street, y'know, where Saks Fifth Avenue used to be—until about a few minutes ago!"

P Is for Playboy: A handsome young playboy showed up at his favorite bistro swathed in bandages. "What happened to you?" asked a friend. "I held up a train," said the playboy. "You?" exclaimed his friend. "Held up a train?" "Yeah," came the laconic answer. "It was a bride's train and it seems I held it up too high!"

An amorous playboy had cornered his girl in the back seat of the sedan and was eagerly trying his hand at her. She kept resisting and pushing him away. But still he persisted. Finally, she became annoyed and gave him a violent shove. "Lester," she said, smoothing her skirt which had fallen to the floor during the struggle, "I don't know what's come over you. You've always been so restrained and so gentlemanly." "Yes, I know," said Lester apologetically, "but I just can't help it. I'm trying to give up smoking."

P Is for Poland: In Warsaw, two strangers were standing admiring a brand-new shiny automobile. One exclaimed enthusiastically, "A handsome machine, isn't it? Just another triumphant exhibit of Soviet ingenuity and initiative." The other man said, "But that's an American car. Can't you tell one when you see one? Didn't you know that?" and the other one said, "Yes, I knew it, but I don't know you!"

P Is for Politics: Franklin D. Roosevelt, Jr. claims that this is the most popular joke sweeping the political corridors in Washington. Senators Lyndon Johnson, Jack Kennedy and Stu Symington were swapping chitchat in the Senate lunchroom when the latter said: "I had a real nice dream last night. I dreamed that God touched me on the back and said, 'Stu, you are going to be the next President of the United States.'" "That's a coincidence," Kennedy interrupted. "I had almost the identical dream. I dreamed that God touched me on the back and said, 'John, I have decided that you will be President.'" Johnson, who remained silent through this exchange of dream talk, finally smiled and offered a comment. "I hate to spoil your dreams," he said, "but I think I ought to tell you that I wasn't near enough to touch either of you on the back last night!"

A politician was making a speech about the conservation of natural resources. "I'd be willing to wager that there isn't a person in this crowd who has done a single thing to help conserve our timber." No one spoke for a few seconds. Then, a meek-looking fellow in the back stood up, raised his hand and said, "I once shot a woodpecker."

"What do you think is to blame for all our problems with the countries in Europe?" asked the interviewer of the Senator. "The trouble with American foreign relations," replied the Senator, "is that they're all broke."

A member of Congress insisted that he never made a mistake. "I'm always right," he told an associate, "and furthermore, I'd rather be right than President." "Don't worry," smiled his companion, "you'll never be either."

P Is for Poor: There is one good thing about being poor—it's inexpensive.

P Is for Psychiatrist: Not too long ago I was feeling quite distraught and nervous, whatever that means, so I went to visit my psychiatrist. He said to me, "Joey, give up smoking." I said, "Why?" He said, "Listen to me, Joey, give up smoking!" I said, "What for? It's not bad for me." He said, "I know, but you're burning my couch. . . ."

This fellow awoke one morning and discovered lilies growing right out of the top of his head. He ran straight down to his psychiatrist's office. The head shrinker stared at the flowers. He said, "Why, this is fantastic. Now where on earth do you suppose those flowers came from?" The guy yelled, "Look at the card! See who sent them!"

A man dressed in mid-eighteenth-century garb approached a psychiatrist and told him, "I'm Abraham Lincoln." Then he whispered, "Doc, I've got a serious problem. I think my wife's trying to get rid of me. She keeps insisting that I take her to the theatre."

A man visited a psychiatrist because he thought he was Colonel Nasser. The head shrinker assured him that it wasn't too serious a delusion. "A lot you know," moaned the man. "I happen to be Jewish."

A psychiatrist was explaining to her patient, "Now, you mustn't continually say you're Adam. It's just nonsense and an absurdity of your mind. You couldn't have been the first man." "Skip the long talk, Doc, that's what caused all the trouble between me and my wife."

A fellow ran into a psychiatrist's office and told the head shrinker, "My girl friend thinks she's a rabbit." "Bring her in," suggested the dome doctor. "I think I can help." "You certainly can," said the man. "If she comes to see you, don't cure her."

Young man to psychiatrist: "My trouble is, I'm from Texas —and I'm ashamed of it."

A very distraught businessman went to a psychiatrist and told him that he was very jumpy and upset and couldn't sleep nights. "I've got a plan," said the psychiatrist. "Where do you live?"

"The Bronx."

"All right. How do you get to work?"

"I take the subway."

"You'll have to stop. Here's what you do: get yourself a hoop and a stick and every morning roll the hoop in to work and every night roll the hoop home."

"Isn't that a little silly?"

"A little, but it will give you something to do, keep your mind occupied and tire you physically so you'll sleep."

"Okay, I'll try anything."

The next morning, he rolled his hoop into work and that evening he rolled it home. He kept it up for two weeks and began to feel better. He ate better and slept very well. One day when he went to the garage where he parked his hoop, the attendant greeted him with a long face. Since the attendant had a long face anyway, the businessman wasn't worried. However, the attendant said, "Mr. Jones, I have bad news for you. Some guy came in here driving a big Cadillac and before we could stop him he ran over your hoop."

"Oh," said the man, "that's awful. How'm I going to get home?"

One chap had a distinct fear of telephones—when they rang, he just wouldn't answer. But the psychiatrist took care of that. After considerable analysis the man was cured. Now he answers the phone whether it rings or not.

A beautiful girl walked into the psychiatrist's office and he leaped at her, kissing her with all his lips. When he pulled away he said, "Well, that takes care of my problems, now what's on *your* mind?"

"Do you believe in child psychiatry?" asked a troubled man. "Yes, I do," said his friend. "Why don't you visit mine, he's only eleven years old."

Q Is for Quiet:

"Dear, what in the world did we use to do back home, before *we got our television set?"*

Q Is for Questions: An elderly lady was introduced to Dr. Klein at a party. At her first opportunity she cornered the gentleman and said, "Doctor, I'm so glad to meet you. Let me ask you a question. Lately I get a terrible pain here in my side when I raise my arm like this. What should I do about it?" The gentleman answered, "I'm very sorry, madam, but you see I'm not that kind of a doctor. I happen to be a doctor of economics." "Oh," said the old lady. "So tell me, Doctor, should I sell my General Motors?"

A man was seen walking around on a very warm day wearing a heavy overcoat. A friend stopped him and asked why he was doing such an obviously silly thing. "My dear friend," answered the perspiring fellow, "there are some things you and I know. There are some things only I know. There are some things only God knows. That I am wearing a heavy overcoat on a hot day, you know and I know. That I have a big hole in the seat of my pants only I know. And when it will be fixed, only God knows!"

"Dad," asked the boy, "what's the difference between 'anger' and 'exasperation'?" "Well," answered the father, "it's mostly a matter of degree. Suppose I show you an example and then you won't forget." The father went to the telephone and dialed a number at random. To the man who answered the phone, he said, "Hello, is Boris there?" The man answered, "Mister, there's no Boris here. Won't you please look up the number before you dial?" The father turned to his son. "See?" he pointed out. "That man wasn't a bit happy with our call. He was probably very busy with something and we annoyed him. Now watch . . ." He dialed the number again. "Hello," said the father calmly, "is Boris there?" "Now look here!" came the heated reply, "you just called this number and I told you there's no Boris here! You've a lot of nerve calling again. You better look up the right number this time!" The receiver slammed hard. The father turned to his son and said, "You see, son, that was anger. Now I'll show you what 'exasperation' means." He again dialed the same number, and when a violent voice roared "HELLO," the father calmly said, "Hello, this is Boris. Any calls for me?"

QUESTIONS AND ANSWERS: Marriage?—Declaration of War.
Divorce?—Declaration of Peace.
Alimony?—Taxation without
Representation.

Q Is for Quiz: When a quizmaster asked a contestant, "If you win this $500, what are you going to do with it?" the contestant said, *"Count it!"*

Have you ever noticed that few chorus girls go to Quiz shows? That's because they can always get a mink coat by merely answering only ONE question!

A contestant was asked on a Quiz show to name some famous Russells. The contestant said, "Lillian" and the quizmaster said, "That's one"; and the contestant continued and said "Jane" and the Quiz Emcee said, "That's three . . ."

They have a new twist in Quiz shows now—they call you up and if you are home, they borrow $20 from you.

Q Is for Quotations: The ten best years in a woman's life come between 28 and 30.

A woman's word is never done.

A man is only as old as he looks—and if he only looks, he's old.

Pretty soon all the drive-in theaters will be open and people will quit watching movies again.

I've got the sun in the morning and the father at night.

Gee, but it's great to be shot by a pal.

Do unto others before they do unto you.

French actor Maurice Chevalier telling how it feels to be seventy: "It's not so bad—especially when you consider the alternative."

Novelist Somerset Maugham, commenting on British cooking: "If you want to eat well in England, eat three breakfasts daily."

R Is for Race Tracks: Duke Zeibert, a restaurateur in Washington, D.C., served me this: Now they have a special window for the women bettors—a $1.98 window.

I have a system to beat the first four races at the track every day—don't show up till the fifth.

R Is for Real Estate:

"Not much . . . attic space!"

I don't play the horses for money. I play strictly for laughs. Last week I laughed away my car and my home. . . .

R Is for Railroads: On a certain railroad whose trains were notoriously late and slow, a young woman passenger gave birth to a baby. It took the entire staff and most of the facilities to bring her and the child through. When the ordeal was over and the mother and child were resting in one of the drawing rooms, the conductor finally gave vent to his annoyance. He said, "Young lady, you never should have boarded this train knowing you were in that condition." The young mother said, "Sir, I'll have you know that when I got on this train, I was not in that condition."

A district railroad superintendent always made a special point of insisting that all station masters send in an immediate report of any accident, no matter how small it might be. One morning he got a message: *Man fell from station platform in front of moving train. Details later.* He sweated it out for good until he got the second message which read: *Everything okay, nobody hurt ... engine going backwards.*

R Is for Real Estate: A sign in front of a real estate office: WE HAVE LOTS TO BE THANKFUL FOR!

This afternoon I went over to the real estate office to see a model home but she had already left.

When a real estate agent asked a woman if she wanted to buy a home, she said, "What do I need a home for? I was born in a hospital, educated in a college, courted in an automobile and married in a church. I live out of paper bags and delicatessen stores. I spend my mornings at the golf course, my afternoons at the bridge table and my evenings at the movies. And when I die, I'm gonna be buried at the undertaker's. I don't need a home—all I need is a garage!"

R Is for Relations: He's my own flesh and blood—he's got the flesh and I got the blood.

R Is for Restaurant: A gal ordered a filet mignon, the most expensive dish on Henry Stampler's menu. The waiter looked at her escort and said, "What do you wish, sir?" "I wish I hadn't brought her," moaned the guy.

Two men wandered into Chez Vito for dinner and ordered the most expensive dishes and the finest champagne. They looked well groomed but they didn't have a penny between them. When the check arrived, one said to the other, "Let's split the check—you wash and I'll dry."

When a customer complained to the waiter that the chicken he served him had one leg shorter than the other, the waiter said, "Look, are you gonna eat it or rhumba with it?"

The chef told Jack E. Leonard: "I put my heart into this clam chowder." Jack snapped, "Never mind your heart—put a few clams into it."

That restaurant is so high class, they even pick up the check with a fork.

I told the waiter I didn't like the looks of the codfish and he said, "If it's looks you want, why don't you order goldfish?"

When I ordered some Russian dressing, they brought me a picture of Khrushchev putting on his pants.

I said, "Hey, waiter, how long did these eggs boil?" and he said, "Five seconds." I said, "Five seconds? But I want 3-minute eggs." He said, "I'm sorry, the chef can't hold them in the water for 3 minutes—burns his hand!"

The restaurant is so swanky, before you use the finger bowls you have to wash your hands.

The Stage Delicatessen does such a terrific business they are now calling it "Fort Lox."

The food is so bad there, instead of a check, the waiter gives you a citation.

I asked him how much was the Nova Scotia salmon. He said, "$7.50 an order." I said, "Look, I wanna buy some salmon—not Nova Scotia."

R Is for Riches: Max Abrams, of Emerson Radios, TV, etc., turned on this one: And then there was the sultan who bought a Cadillac. He paid for it with a ten-thousand-dollar bill and said, "Give me my change in Volkswagens."

It's easy to spot a rich man at a football game. He's the guy who brings an electric blanket.

R Is for Rock 'n' Roll: Harry Waxman, the philanthropist, donated this: Rock 'n' roll music makes me long for the good old days of radio when all you got was static.

R Is for Romania: In Europe they have a new form of tax collection. In Romania, a girl in Bucharest heard the door-bell ring and when she opened the door she saw the tax collector, so she shouted to her mother upstairs, "Ma, the tax collector is here." And her mother shouted, "I'll be right down, give him a chair." The girl shouted back, "A chair won't do, he wants *all* the furniture!"

R Is for Rooster: A rooster found a hole in the fence and crawled through into the next farm. It was an ostrich farm and there were many nests there. He walked over, looked into one and noticed that some ostrich eggs were at least ten times as big as any he'd ever seen. He went back to his farm, got all his hens together and took them back with him. He led them to the nest, pointed and said, "Ladies, I didn't bring you here to scold you and I don't want to sound unreasonable, but I just wanted to show you what's going on in the world outside our farm."

S Is for Safari: Hunter misses—lion leaps—hunter ducks—lion runs away. Hunter goes back to camp and practices shooting. Goes after lion—finds him in a small clearing, practicing short leaps.

S Is for St. Peter: St. Peter was interviewing a pretty girl at the Pearly Gates. "While you were on earth," he asked, "did you indulge in necking, petting, smoking, dancing—" "Never! Never!" she roared emphatically. "Then why haven't you reported sooner?" asked St. Peter. "You've been dead a long time."

S Is for Salary: The salary we used to dream of is the one we can't live on today.

S Is for Science: My outline for a science-fiction tragedy. It concerns a hero who falls in love with an electronic brain, then ends up in jail. Seems he had to rob a bank so he could keep paying her electric bills. . . .

S Is for Scram:

"SCRAM!"

You know this is the age of science and one of its newest discoveries is an electric car; you plug it in a socket in your house and the other end in your car. I know one fellow who did this and traveled all the way from California to New York, and didn't spend a cent for gas—but it cost him four thousand dollars and twenty-six cents. He had to get a long cord. . . .

S Is for Scotland: I don't believe the sick sick story of the Scotsman who murdered his parents so he could go to the orphan's picnic.

In Scotch restaurants they heat the knives so you can't use too much butter.

They stopped the crime wave in Scotland by putting up a sign over the jailhouse saying: ANYONE CAUGHT AND PUT IN JAIL WILL HAVE TO PAY HIS BOARD AND LODGING.

In Scotland they had to take the "Pay-as-you-leave" cars off the streets; they found two Scotsmen starved in one of them.

Scotland—where the cows give condensed milk.

In Scotland, all horse races are very close.

When you ask a Scotch girl if she's free for any night, she's bound to say, "No, but I'll be reasonable."

Scotland, where they borrow a pipeful of tobacco and then can't light it because it's packed too tight.

London isn't the only town that gets foggy in Great Britain. They say it was so foggy in Scotland one day a Scotsman milked three cows before he found out he wasn't playing the bagpipes.

You can always tell when you're flying over Scotland—*No garbage cans.*

The way they teach a Scotsman to swim in Scotland in one lesson: they pin a dollar bill to his bathing suit and throw him in the water.

Please don't misunderstand—some of my closest friends are Scotsmen.

S Is for Secretary: An energetic secretary came into her office, smiled at a co-worker and asked, "And how are you this lovely morning?" Her friend, who'd had a bad night, raised her head slowly and said, "What you need is a good case of tired blood."

S Is for Siberia: The dogs in Siberia are the fastest in the world. That's because the trees are so far apart.

S Is for Sick Jokes: The kid came home from school crying, "Mommy, the teacher said I look like a monkey." "Shut up!" his mother hollered. "And comb your face."

S Is for Signs: Sign in a Hollywood charm school—THINK MINK.

Sign posted in a midtown New York office: THE EASIEST WAY TO MAKE ENDS MEET IS TO GET OFF YOUR OWN.

Sign in a brassière shop: WE FIX FLATS.

Sign in a French antique shop in New York: ENGLISH AND FRENCH SPOKEN—CASH UNDERSTOOD.

S Is for Snob: A snobbish Park Avenue matron walked into a pet shop and ordered the proprietor to give her the finest dog he had in the store. He showed her several of his prize animals but she was dissatisfied. Finally, he picked up an adorable little pup and handed it to her. "Is he pedigreed?" she asked haughtily. "Pedigreed?" smiled the dealer. "If this dog could talk, he wouldn't speak to either of us."

A haughty socialite died and arrived at the gates of Heaven. "Welcome," St. Peter greeted him, "come right in." "I will not," sneered the snob, "any place where a perfect stranger can get in without a reservation is not my idea of Heaven."

S Is for South America: South America has so many revolutions, the Cabinet meets in a revolving door.

My advice to any South American president—"Don't have any personal stationery made."

Things are so quiet in South America, it's about time we sent Vice-President Nixon down there on another good-will tour.

S Is for South Pole: Two penguins from the South Pole were madly in love with each other and they had planned to get married, but somehow they got separated. Finally, at Christmastime, one penguin received a telegram from the other that read: MERRY XMAS, I AM WITH BYRD.

S Is for Spain: A modern neurotic is a guy who doesn't build castles in Spain. He builds ranch houses there.

In an arena in Spain one angry bull came charging out of the pen. The bullfighter raised a green cape and waved it wildly at the bull. "What are you doing?" shouted a man in the grandstand. "What's the idea of a green cloth? If you want the bull to charge, you should use a red cloth." The matador looked up and shook his head. "Red makes him stop. This bull was raised by an American traffic cop."

S Is for Speaker: The speaker had agreed to address the monthly meeting of a small but active group of nice elderly ladies. The evening turned out to be miserable—one of those snow-sleet-wind combinations that make home-sweet-home seem even sweeter than usual. Arriving at the scheduled time, the speaker found the meeting only halfway through its agenda. He sat politely by while the ladies reported at length on their activities. After an hour or so, the chairlady called the business meeting to a close, and in a formal and dramatic voice announced, "Ladies, we want to welcome our guest speaker. We've to appreciate that he is with us. Not even a dog would go out on such a night and he did it!

"This man," she stated with sincerity and enthusiasm, "is a true example of sacrifice and courage. Nothing has been too much for him. Call him late at night and with no notice at all, he's on a plane traveling hundreds of miles to cover a meeting. Ask him for help of any kind and he's right on the spot. As a matter of fact, I don't know how he keeps it up—he must have a heart of granite!"

And believe it or not, at another meeting on the same day, a committee was deciding on a speaker for an important national conference. Several suggestions were made but none seemed to fill the bill properly. Finally, in some exasperation and complete innocence, the chairman observed, "Well, it certainly is hard to pinhead the speaker."

S Is for Square: Lou Barnett, of Loma Plastics, angled in with this: My idea of a square is a guy who goes to a Brigitte Bardot movie and complains because the picture doesn't have a plot.

S Is for Squelch: A Bostonian visited San Antonio, Texas, and asked a native, "What is that dilapidated-looking ruin over there?" "That, suh, is the Alamo. In that building, suh, 136 immortal Texans held off an army of 15,000 of Santa Ana's regulars for four days." "Um-m-m," said the Bostonian, "and who was that man on horseback on that hill over there?" "That, suh, is a statue of a Texas ranger. He killed 46 Apaches in singlehanded combat and broke up 47 riots in his lifetime. Where you from, stranger?" "I'm from Boston. We have our heroes there, too. Paul Revere, for instance—" "Paul Revere!" snorted the Texan. "You mean that man who had to ride for help?"

Any comedian worth his weight in laughs should be able to handle a heckler, on or off stage, at the drop of a gag. Your proper line can be a rope around the neck of your opponent if it's used at the right place at the right time. Here are some good squelchers to be put away in your brain file, so that you will always be prepared for battle:

I couldn't warm up to you if we were cremated together.

It isn't that we have anything against you personally—you just happen to be the kind of jerk we don't want hanging around the premises.

You may be a social lion to your friends but you're just an animal cracker to me.

Why don't you gargle concrete and let it get hard?

What a combination—corny and illiterate.

You're the sort of guy who talks penthouses and takes subways.

He's the kind of guy who picks his friends—to pieces.

They're about as compatible as ham and matzoths.

He's an intellectual. He can bore you on every subject.

You're snappy on the comeback—like your checks.

Don't you ever get tired of having yourself around?

Stay with me. I want to be alone.

Why don't you send your wits out to be sharpened?

Are you a self-made man, or do you want to blame someone else?

Why don't you go on a diet and quit eating my heart out?

There was something I always liked about him—but he spent it.

His idea of an exciting night is to turn up his electric blanket.

Most of our top-drawer actors are amiable folks, approachable, tolerant, often eager to help newcomers. The old-timers held themselves more aloof. Perhaps the most irascible, sharp-spoken was the late Wilton Lackaye—a great performer but not the most amiable gentleman. Once, after his opening night in *The Pit,* he came into the Lambs Club and was approached by an eager young hopeful who exclaimed enthusiastically, "How does it feel, Mr. Lackaye, to receive all that wild acclaim for your great acting?" Lackaye stared at him coldly and snapped: "You'll never know!"

S Is for Stupid: You want her to write Happy Birthday on the cake. For three hours she tries to get the cake into the typewriter.

S Is for Suburbs: An American city is a place where by the time you've finished paying for your home in the suburbs, the suburbs have moved 20 miles farther out.

S Is for Switch: Here are two versions of Garbo's famous sayings:

1—During the shooting of one of her most memorable films, the great G.G. found herself slightly short of cash. Accordingly, she went to her bank, stepped up to the teller and told him, "I vant for me a loan."

2—The great G.G. walked into a hotel and stepped up to the desk clerk. The fellow recognized her and was very solicitous. "Just sign the register, Miss Garbo," he told her, "and I'm sure you'll be well satisfied with your room. By the way, would you like a room with a bath in it?" Garbo glared at him and acidly said, "No! I vant to be alone."

When Jerry Lee Lewis, the singer, married a thirteen-year-old girl, Bob Hope cracked, "He just became a father—he adopted his wife." . . . Cindy said, "She can't be with him for the next three months, she's going to camp for the summer."

S Is for Switzerland: Two Cincinnati sightseers were mountain climbing in the Swiss Alps when they lost their way, somehow. 'Midst the drifts of ice and snow they yoo-hoo'd, holloo'd and yodeled. Nothing happened; for hours they wandered. They roamed so long even the guarantees on their Swiss watches were used up. Then from around the corner came a St. Bernard, dragging a beaker of cognac around his neck. "Hallelujah," cried one, "we're saved. Here comes man's best friend." "Yeah, and look at the size of the dog carrying it."

When I was in Switzerland, I saw a big Swiss Cheese who was such a great ice skater that he had an accountant following him around, adding up his figure eights.

In Geneva the hotels are so ritzy that when you request fresh milk in the dining room, they bring the goat to your table.

Sign in Switzerland at one of the resorts: *Attention all skiers. When you break an arm or leg, have your friends write their names on the cast. When you have the cast removed, send same to us and we will transform it into a beautiful indestructible vase or lamp or an umbrella rack and it will be a treasured heirloom possession and souvenir of Switzerland.*

In Switzerland I found out what Swiss cheese really is—just a bunch of holes strung together.

I love Switzerland for its skiing—what a wonderful sport. One day of glorious skiing and six months in the hospital.

A Swiss left his beloved Switzerland for America and opened a jewelry factory in Greenwich Village where he is now making watches with *"Swish"* movements.

In Switzerland there's a man who raises St. Bernard dogs just for the brandy.

T Is for Tailors: A tailor was complaining about his business on account of the warm weather setting in so early when he should be selling heavier garments. He said, "Mine suits are better than money. Money you can get rid of."

My tailor sold me a suit he said would wear like iron, and he's right. I can't even sit down in it!

T Is for Taxes: This is a funny world. If you do wrong you get fined—if you do right you get taxed.

A merchant got into trouble with the income taxers so he went to the office to explain his records which were full of shorthand and mysterious markings. They told him they only wanted to know how much he spent, how much he took in and how much he profited. He said, "That's all? I wouldn't even tell that to mine partner."

T Is for Travel:

"I don't mind being pinched. How about Italy?"

Nowadays we don't make money, we just hold it for the Government between tax collections.

The difference between death and taxes is that death doesn't get worse every time Congress meets!

Ad in newspaper: MAN WITH INCOME TAX BLANK WOULD LIKE TO MEET LADY WITH INCOME.

The tax collector must love poor people, he's creating so many of them.

I wrote the Income Tax Bureau to have a heart, and they wrote back and said, *We'll take it!*

With taxes taking everything, you work like a dog all your life so you can live like a dog.

I found out that it's the Ways and Means committee which takes care of your taxes—if you have the Means they'll find the Ways to get it!

The income tax is the Government's version of *instant poverty.*

T Is for Taxicab: This guy was in a cab. The cab driver said, "Where you wanta go?" The guy answered, "Anywhere." The driver stopped and said, "Get out, I got a schedule to make."

T Is for Teheran: In Teheran when you use the phone you make what is known as Persian to Persian calls.

T Is for Telephone Operator: The meek little man completed the phone call, hung up and then chuckled as his dime clinked back into the slot. Suddenly the telephone rang. "Are you the man who just made a call?" the operator asked. "Well, then, by mistake I returned your dime. Will you please redeposit it?" "Sorry, ma'am," the caller said in a typical telephone operator's monotone. "I can't do that, but if you send me your name and address I'll be glad to send the dime to you in stamps."

T Is for Television: Did you hear about the TV announcer's kid saying his bedtime prayer? The kid said, "Please make me a good boy until my birthday—and now a short commercial about an electric train set."

Some of the late-late movies now being shown on television are pretty old, but it isn't true that all of them were made when movies were first being made. We saw a late-late television movie last night that was made *before* they made movies.

Entertainment is all right for some, but we prefer television programs that make you stop and think. Our favorites are "Network Difficulties" and "One Moment, Please."

The difference between television and vaudeville—in vaudeville, if you lay an egg in Boston, you make up for it by doing well in Providence the following week; but on television, if you lay an egg you lay it all over the country—it's an omelet!

Some of the movies shown on the Late Show and Late Late Show are too old to be kept up that late.

T Is for Theatre: I've always had the theatre in my veins—sometimes I wish I had blood.

My advice to stage-struck young ladies who want to break into show business: Change your hair style, learn how to walk, buy a sexy wardrobe and before you know it—you'll be married and have 6 kids and forget all about the mishmash.

The theatre is my home. Where else can you get an apartment nowadays?

I know one theatre that would definitely be safe in case of an atomic attack—it never had a hit.

During the height of the vaudeville era when Alexander Pantages owned a chain of theatres, his Salt Lake City theatre was a coveted booking. One song-and-dance team was disgruntled because of losing the Salt Lake booking, so they threatened to cancel the rest of the Pantages bookings and wired Pantages: EITHER PLAY US AT SALT LAKE CITY OR COUNT US OUT. They received the following wire in reply: ONE, TWO, THREE, FOUR, FIVE, SIX, SEVEN, EIGHT, NINE, TEN! ALEXANDER PANTAGES.

T Is for Traffic: The traffic was so bad that rescue planes had to drop supplies and food to the Good-Humor man.

I read where a man is knocked down by a car every five minutes, in traffic. That guy must be made of iron.

The only time a pedestrian has the right of way is in an ambulance on the way to the hospital.

A rookie cop was asked by his Sergeant what he was doing away from his corner where he was supposed to be directing traffic. He said, "I want another corner, Sarge. The traffic at my corner is always getting balled up."

T Is for Trailers: Ben Goldman, the eagle in Eagle Clothes, fitted me with this: The guy who invented the trailer probably got the idea from his grandmother's bustle, because it's something that's tied on behind.

T Is for Travel: After looking at a prospective tourist's passport photo, a fellow at a travel bureau commented, "If the owner really looks like that, he's too sick to travel."

I heard that Washington is so economy-minded these days that Vice-President Nixon is flying tourist.

When my wife packs for a trip, the only thing she leaves behind is a note for the milkman.

T Is for Turkey: They must have a girl's ball team in the Sultan's harem. One day one of the girls asked the Sultan if she was in tomorrow's line-up.

The fact that Turkish women are covering their faces only proves that the men don't count on their faces—they rely on figures.

U Is for Useful:

"Don't ask me ... I don't know where they are."

U Is for Ugly: I asked the girl in front of me at the movies to remove her hat. She became very angry. She wasn't wearing any. I liked her face. It reminded me of my home—especially the front stoop. I began talking to her and commented favorably about her wavy hair. Later, I found out that her hair was straight, but her head was wavy.

His second wife is so ugly that two weeks before he took her home he told his children ghost stories so they wouldn't be frightened when they saw her.

She had a real shady background—why not? She had hips like a beach umbrella.

Sylvia had blue eyes, red lips and 13 white teeth. When she smiled, she looked like the Colonial flag. That wasn't bad—but when she laughed she looked like George Washington.

There was one gal named Abigail Schwartz who had a beautiful face except for her nose. She had to lift it up to eat. But a girl's face isn't everything. Listen to this: Abigail's measurements were 38-23-38—those were her leg measurements.

An acquaintance tells of a wise guy husband saying to a visiting friend, "Yes, that was my wife who opened the door for you—do you think I would hire a maid that homely?"

Some girl I never went with was so ugly that when she came into a room the mice jumped on the chairs. She used to model bicycle pumps. And what charm. When she left the room, she gave it an added glow. She was a good dancer, though. They called her "crazy legs." She had four of them. She used to be an Arthur Murray dance instructor but she finally gave it up. She couldn't teach Arthur how to dance. But when you come right down to it (and you had to—she was four feet tall), she had everything a man desires—muscles and a beard.

Her head sticking out of a cellar door would start a hockey game in anybody's neighborhood.

She's so ugly she rents herself out for Halloween parties.

She's so ugly her face looks like it's done up in curlers.

She was too ugly to have her face lifted so they lowered her body instead.

She used to do scarecrow work by appointment only.

If all the girls are sisters under the skin, I wish she'd go back under there and send out her sister.

U Is for Undertakers: He looks as if an undertaker started to work on him and was suddenly called away.

Sign in an undertaker's window: DRIVE CAREFULLY—WE CAN WAIT.

I know an undertaker who even when he goes to the opera, he sits in a box!

When undertakers have a convention they meet on matters of grave importance.

A kid stole a sign from a nursery and stuck it in front of an undertaking parlor. It read: LET US DO YOUR PLANTING FOR YOU.

U Is for University: A university is an institution which has room for 2,000 in the classroom and over 50,000 in the stadium.

A well-known professor kept warning his college students about the perils of sin. "Would you," he asked his class one afternoon, his voice trembling with excitement, "trade a lifetime of peace of mind and happiness for just one hour of wild, animal pleasure?" A soprano voice attached to a pretty thing was heard from the back of the room, "How do you make it last an hour?"

U Is for Used Car Dealer: "Let me put it this way," a used car dealer told a fellow who was trying to sell him his old car. "If your car were a horse, it would have to be shot."

A used car dealer who switched to used TV sales, pitched this line to a customer: "This set's hardly been used. It belonged to an old lady in Westchester with weak eyes."

V Is for Vacation: Where does Lowell Thomas go on his vacation?

V Is for Vaudeville: A vaudeville ventriloquist whose engagements had become fewer and fewer finally dropped off altogether. In desperation the ventriloquist thought of the only possible way he could utilize his talent. He became a spiritualist, using his trick voice, of course, as the ghost's. One night a large bejeweled woman called on the swami. Could he get in touch with her recently departed husband? Could

V Is for Values:

"Sure, the state has a good case—but look what we got on our side—38-24-36."

he! In no time at all, the "spirit" was talking quite animatedly with his delighted wife. When the lights came on, the woman thanked the medium, showered him with praise and asked the charge. "That was the $50 seance," he replied, preening like a peacock. Then he added magnanimously, "For $100, madam, your husband will talk to you while drinking a glass of water."

A small-time vaudeville comic was in a plane crash and awoke to find himself in a strange place. "Where am I?" he asked a fellow standing beside him. "You're in Hell," he was informed. "That's my agent for you," sighed the comic, "he's never booked me in a good spot yet."

A TV salesman was trying to convince a vaudevillian to buy a portable model. "Just imagine," he said, "when you're on tour, sitting in a lonely hotel room, all you have to do is press a button and suddenly a gorgeous, scantily dressed girl will be standing in front of you." "The hotels I stop at," said the ham, "I can get the same thing without television."

W Is for Warning: This is the story about a fellow who shunned American ships to Europe. Against the pleadings of his friends, he took a Russian boat. When told he would regret it, he sardonically replied, "Do me something—what can you do me?" When he was halfway across the ocean, they send him a radiogram to the Commie ship reading: IF YOU CAN'T KNOCK OFF KHRUSHCHEV, GET GROMYKO!

W Is for Westerns: If Horace Greeley were alive in this TV age, he'd probably advise, "Go Western, Young Man. . . ."

I saw a Western on TV so modern that the hero chewed filter-tipped tobacco.

This has been a rough year for Western heroes on TV. Not one of them has made it back to his ranch yet without getting ambushed by a commercial.

I saw a Western on TV last night so old that Gabby Hayes had five-o'clock shadow.

W Is for Watch Out!

"Watch out!"

Jerry Kaufman, of Allside Company of Akron, Ohio, saddled up this one: Nowadays when an American cowboy tells you he's heading for the last roundup, he means his sponsor didn't pick up his option.

A modern cowboy doesn't have to know how to rope a steer as long as he knows how to rope a sponsor.

I saw a Western on TV last night so adult that the gambling house owner didn't lose his life for running a crooked game—he lost his license.

I saw a Western on TV last night so adult that they didn't let Billy the Kid in the saloon because he was under twenty-one.

I saw a Western on TV last night so modern that the saloon had a press agent.

I saw a Western on TV last night so modern the Indians couldn't burn down the settlement because their lighters weren't working.

W Is for Who's Who: In Russia there are two editions of Who's Who. One is called Who Was Who; the other is called Who Is Still Who.

W Is for Wife: My wife has been affected by the latest fads. Every time I ask her to do something she says, "Do it yourself!"

W Is for Will: The old man was dictating his will. "To my son," he said, "I leave one hundred thousand. To my daughter—one hundred thousand. To my grandson—ten thousand. To my granddaughter—ten thousand." The lawyer interrupted, "But sir, you only have three thousand dollars." The old man growled, "Let them go out and work for a living like I did."

W Is for Wolf: The wolf at the bar was trying to make time with a gorgeous creature whose dress was bursting at the seams, which is as good a place as any. "Oh," said the babe, who had been around more than a carousel, "I bet your wife doesn't understand you." "She understands me all right," said the gent, "it's just that she's fat and ugly."

W Is for Work: One workingman down on his luck griped to a fellow worker: "It just doesn't figure. Here I am born in America and I can't make a living. Sam has been here only three years and already owes $600,000!"

W Is for Wrestling: On TV recently, a wrestler was tossed out of the ring and came up in pain. The excited ring announcer actually yelled, "This part is on the level!"

X Is for Xperts:

X Is for Xmas: A young soldier was depressed. In the spirit of the holidays, I asked him, "Wasn't Santa Claus good to you?" "Good to me?" he said sadly. "Twenty years ago I asked Santa Claus for a soldier suit—and now I get it!"

I love to shop at Gimbel's around Xmas because everybody is so polite and helpful. One woman broke her leg while shopping and they gift-wrapped it.

The burglars and pickpockets association of Madison Avenue have asked me to announce that there are just 36 more shop-lifting days till Xmas.

You can tell that Xmas is approaching. Macy's has just captured Gimbel's first comparison shopper. And Gimbel's retaliated by capturing a Macy Santa Claus—a prisoner exchange is being worked out now.

Xmas is the time of the year to get the kids something for the old man to play with.

I'm writing to Santa Claus early this Xmas to tell him what I want—how do you spell Brigitte Bardot?

I'm getting my girl a fountain pen for Xmas as a surprise, and wotta surprise it's gonna be—she expects a Cadillac.

My uncle did his Xmas shopping early and what do you think he got? Thirty days!

Y Is for Yokels: I know a yokel farmer who married a girl so young he comes in from the fields three or four times a day just to see if his wife came home from school yet.

A yokel was on trial for killing his wife when he caught her with a neighbor, and when he was asked why he shot her instead of her lover, he said, "Aw shucks, ah'd rather shoot a woman once than a man every week."

The teacher in a small country school was explaining some arithmetic problems when she noticed the class yokel, a tall gangly lad, the dopiest pupil in school, watching rather

Y Is for Yes, Dear:

"Never mind why. . . . Just you bury your head in the sand."

intently. She was happy to know that at last he was beginning to understand. When she finished, she said to him, "Cicero, you look so interested. I'm sure you want to ask some questions." And Cicero got up and drawled, "Waaaal, ma'am, I got one t'ask. Where do them numbers go when yew rub 'em off th'board?"

Y Is for Youth: The best way for a girl to keep her youth— is not to introduce him to anyone.

I think that every woman should hold on to her youth but not while he's driving.

You know a boy is growing up when he stops wanting to go out with girls and wants to stay home with them.

Z Is for Zoo: A father took his son to the zoo and pointed out the lions to him and said, "Son, there is the most ferocious of all animals. If he should ever get out of that cage, he would tear me to pieces." The kid said, "Papa, if he should, what number bus should I take to get home?"

She's so dumb she went to the zoo to see what a Christmas seal looks like.

She's always attracted to the zoo because she heard that all men are beasts and she just loves animals.

The new lion in the zoo was fed a few bananas, while the old lion in the adjoining cage was fed big chunks of red meat. The new lion finally asked the older lion, "How come I only get bananas while you get steak?" "This zoo," explained the old lion, "works on a low budget and they've got you registered as a monkey."

The beautiful girl was one candidate for the job at the zoo as a lion tamer. The other was an eager young man. The manager said he would give them both a chance, and told the girl to go into the cage. The girl, wearing a big fur coat, did so. The huge lion was let in with her and he immediately started to charge at her. Suddenly she stood upright, opened

Z Is for Zulu:

her fur coat and stood there, completely naked. The lion stopped dead, spun around and went meekly back to the corner. The manager was properly amazed. He turned toward the young man. "Well, pal, do you think you can top that?" "I'd like to try," said the guy, "just get that crazy lion out of there."

Z Is for Zoology: An absent-minded professor was conducting a class in zoology and addressing the students. He said, "Now students, this morning we will take this frog apart and see what makes him croak." And he took a paper bag out of his pocket, then emptied the contents on his desk. Out rolled a ham sandwich. He scratched his head and said, "Mmm, now that's funny. I distinctly remember eating my lunch!"

THE ADAMS APPENDIX

LIKE all married men I have a wife. Unlike all married men I love my wife. I am very happy. I am brainwashed.

My Cindy is a writer. She'd rather write than eat . . . and with her cooking we're better off. My Cindy is a columnist for the national theatrical weekly *Showbusiness.* Her humorous articles, features, and series have been printed—if not read— in the country's leading newspapers and magazines. She is talented. She is hard-working and she is handsomely paid—if you call a buck an article good-looking. She says I am the only person who's ever taken what she has to offer without paying her. This is true. It's just that I haven't found out which one of all the things she does for me deserves the payment.

Cindy says (which also happens to be the title of her scratchings) that jokes and joke books are written for men. Men buy them, men read them and, unless there are big words, men tell them.

Cindy says women can be funny, too. With this I agree. Anybody who's ever seen a nearsighted female apply make-up knows how funny they can be.

Some women can't laugh at themselves, but Cindy is the type that will sit around laughing at herself all day. You might think this is embarrassing when guests come over, but no one can really hear her from the closet. Her little mind is always percolating, and she is able to see her own private blend of humor in almost anything. Since I am forced, by a previous contract (our marriage license), to include some of Cindy's columns in this book, I may as well admit that I think you can learn something from her peculiar, perceptive perspective in plucking the humor out of life. To her, life is just a bowl of jolly.

Therefore, without benefit of salary but with benefit of clergy, I hereby introduce my wife, my personal court jester, Cindy Adams, whose oddball commentaries have giggled me into Tiffany's credit department and entertained me many a time on that long, dreary elevator ride up to Bergdorf Goodman's fur department. . . .

Cindy Says . . .

"Glamor girls in show business gotta watch they don't gain weight," my husband said, depleting a vatful of spaghetti. Since I was already having difficulty wriggling my size-eight body into the size-seven wardrobe, I realized it was time to do or diet. The next day, I decided, I'd begin.

Came the next day I decided I'd begin the next day. I immediately began eating like the Government had proclaimed rationing. I threw proteins to the wind and began inhaling carbohydrates and starches at a rapid rate. Potatoes became my main dish. (This was unusually gluttonous since I despise potatoes.) Between shovelfuls I allayed everyone's fears with "Tomorrow I start dieting." My refrigerator raids made D-Day look like slow motion. Even seeing Betty Furness on television made my tummy develop a nervous tic.

A tempting part in summer stock was the straw that broke the Operation Avoirdupois. I lumbered on the scale, cursed the manufacturer for its inaccuracy and commenced with grapefruit and yogurt instead of pancakes and syrup. I followed with black iced coffee and a red-hot blast at my husband. I find it strenuous being cheerful on eight hundred calories.

Martyred, I disdained lunch. By midafternoon I was so hungry that I relished the Bufferins I took for the resultant migraine. Dinner couldn't make an amoeba burp and at bedtime my stomach's demands for attention were met with a quarter of an apple.

Before retiring I offered the scale another chance to redeem itself. It revealed I hadn't lost a gram all day. I was positive it was imperfectly balanced and the manufacturers were perfectly unbalanced and that the whole thing was a plot against me.

Finally I visited a masseuse who patted, rolled and massaged me out of ten bucks. She diagnosed my problem as water retention. I diagnosed hers as poverty. For five treatments at fifty dollars per week for three years, she guaranteed she could solve my problem—and hers! Figures I had water in my body . . . I sure didn't have any food.

Now, besides cutting down on solids, I had to limit my liquids. Condiments, too, since salt retains fluid. It got so I dined sumptuously on nonsweetened dried prunes and dietetic boiled carrots. When entertaining company, I'd toss in some spinach . . . for an appetizer!

One week later I became listless, apathetic and waxen. Specialists were consulted, X-rays were taken, tests were tested and they prescribed a sanitarium. I didn't need a sanitarium. I needed a sandwich. I was s-t-a-r-v-i-n-g !

Since I couldn't relinquish food, I tried other methods. I went bicycle riding and horseback riding. I mailed twenty-five cents and a stamped, self-addressed envelope for a booklet entitled "Obesity And Who Needs It." I even investigated Slenderella, Maclevy and Gayelord Hauser's jazz.

These salons gave me hot steam baths, icy showers and alcohol rubs. I was fat but clean! I suffered in weight-reducing machines that shake, knead and scrape off flesh and "break the fatty cholesterol deposits or your money refunded (not cheerfully)." What those vibrators broke was some blood vessels, a blister on my leg and my spirit. They can keep the money. Let them refund my leg.

This exertion didn't help because it was so enervating I'd eat wolfishly afterwards, thereby regaining what I'd just lost. Slogans like *A second on the lip, a lifetime on the hip* spurred

me onward and at one point I lost five pounds overnight . . .
I dropped my wallet!

Finally, ounce by ounce, I pulled myself out of the cottage-
cheese world where I was living and emerged victorious. I
presented my thin, svelte self to the summer stock producer,
who uttered these immortal, heart-warming words: "The part
calls for a fatter girl!"

As summer reared its head and temperature, "Leave us
vacation," sez I to my husband, one of the last of the red-hot
spenders. Ohhh, I don't mean Aly Khan or Trujillo Jr. have
got to worry, but amongst us white trash he's considered a
very large sport. So, fingering the safety chain on his pocket,
he sez, "What should we do?" Sez I to him, "How's about
cluttering up the Riviera? Or Miami? Or a Caribbean
cruise?" No answer from the Minister of Finance. I lowered
my sights. "I'll settle for a beach club in Connecticut. . . .
Never mind, just fix the air conditioner!"

Crowed Joey, "Pack. We're Jamaica bound." The Jamaica
I figured he was springing for is a Long Island suburb a 15-
cent subway shlep from town and the only thing you gotta
pack for that is a lunch box. "No," sez he, brandishing two
Avianca Airline tickets, "Jamaica BWI not Jamaica, L.I."
Seems Avianca, via our travel agent, Phil Schweidel, tested
Joey's I.Q. and I ain't saying what happened. . . . I can only
tell you the dear husband flew half fare.

Six hours, two meals and one cocktail time later our big-
bellied plane unloaded its big-bellied-loaded humans in
Kingston, whereupon the local Avianca agent entered flitting
insecticide. They're very chintzy about Americans not passing
anything around—except their dollars.

Photogs, reporters and The Honorable Abe Issa, Jamaica
Tourist Board chairman, welcomed us. While I checked pass-
ports, luggage, hand baggage and arrangements, The Big Star
grinned from ear to ear into cameras . . . any cameras. Some
lay on a FOR SALE counter and he beamed wildly into those,
too. Next day's Kingston *Gleaner* immortalized him leering
so maniacally it looked like his throat was cut. When I finally

forced his jaws shut we took off. Past Issa's department stores, Issa's Hardware Co., Issa's Glass Bucket Saloon, Issa's race track, Issa's Chrysler Agency, Issa's Haberdashers, Issa's Free Port Shop, we pulled into Issa's Myrtle Bank Hotel. Clearly, I'd discovered what means BWI—British West Issa.

After vacuuming up whatever straw goods I could beg, borrow or mooch my husband out of, we motored to Ocho Rios. En route I chomped native sugar cane while the dear husband chewed Tums. Joey's concept of sightseeing is to get an air-conditioned suite and have lamb chops sent up. He's infiltrated several continents, but the only sights he's ever seen are some old tired-looking room service waiters. 'Twas here Joey went outdoorsy and commenced Operation Sunburn. Greasing up like for the channel swim he lay in the sun, under the moon, near somebody's lighter, behind a couple of fireflies . . . and for days thereafter he resembled a jelly apple in Bermuda shorts . . . and segued back to the air-conditioning–lamb chops routine.

Early one morning at the break of noon we hired an auto to drag to Montego Bay, the playground of ye classy social set, because, natch, there ain't nobody more classy or socialer than I and my husband. Jamaica, being British, they drive on the left. In America so does Joey. In Jamaica he hugged the right closer than Eddie does Liz. The two-hour drive extolled by travel books as "a heavenly island experience which you won't soon forget" was an experience, all right—and I won't soon forget it. Obviously the gent what wrote it never met Wrong Way Adams, the Barney Oldfield of the AAA.

Bay Roc, which bore up under the thrill of housing such famous guests as we (I discovered later Montego caters to such unknowns as Noel Coward, Oscar Hammerstein, Gable, Errol Flynn and some dukes and ducklings of assorted shapes, sizes and dukedoms), gave us rooms which opened right onto the Caribbean. In fact, come high tide we were right in the Caribbean. Montego's Royal Family are Don de Lisser, whose wife Gary's a NY society portrait painter and his Britttttttttt-tish-speaking nevview John Pringle, whose Liz modeled until

Harper's shipped her to Jamaica on location. They entertained us in their quaint little cottages of 50 or 60 rooms
which overlook their banana, coconut, sugar cane, mango and
money plantations and with their 8 servants who earn, com-
bined, $45 per week. I considered mumbling, "I got a lovely
four-room apartment with a terrace on 5th Avenue and one
part-time maid" but I didn't because I can't stand pity.

Our vacation was delicious and I don't even mind that
Generous Joe made me chip in. For a jazzy few days we lived
à la Queen Elizabeth & Whatsisname. True, we blew all our
capital, but it was worth it . . . even if now I hafta struggle
along the rest of the summer with a busted air conditioner. . . .

Our pioneers struggled through hardships like Indians,
plagues, roll your own cigarettes—and without a thinking
man's filter, yet. Still they were happier than we. Mebbe effen
a Cherokee trimmed 'em too close they had headaches, but
no psychosomatic ills. No ulcers. No neuroses. Know why?
No TV repairmen.

Recently, our living room set began acting childishly.
Everyone resembled Katharine Hepburn, long and narrow.
Then it belched and the Kate Hepburns became Kate Smiths.
Next, wide, black, twenty-three-inch margins framed our
twenty-four-inch screen thereby diminishing its size to a
Brownie snapshot. This we ignored. Then the sound buzzed
and beeped and fizzled altogether in favor of a Donovan's-
brain type noise which crackled and burbled. This we ignored. Then, my husband Joey appeared on camera looking
like a reflection of those crazy-house mirrors and sounding
like an asthmatic Andy Devine. This, too, we ignored because
he'd never looked or sounded better.

Soon our set began transmitting two channels simultaneously . . . together . . . at the same time. I called the manufacturer. "What's to complain? On popular TV nights this is
a bonus," he hollered and hung up. I bore this until I flicked
on my two-faced set and watched Liberace making love to
Charles Boyer while brother George fiddled around Peter
Lorre. I said good luck to them. I don't care about their pri-

vate lives but who needs it at six o'clock while I'm slaving over a hot husband?

I called a TV repairman. Explained it was an emergency. I can do without riches. I can do without food. I can even do without rich food. But without television? Never! Rather I would face death, the guillotine, the radio—anything! I phoned him bright and early Monday, and nice and late Saturday he arrived. Lucky I said it was an emergency.

He turned on the set, twirled the dials and, as usual, I punched it and kicked it to start it and we both sat back. Worked like a doll.

"Takes a while," I apologized lamely. Hours later the reception was still perfect but we weren't. We were starving. Watching TV makes you hungry so the repairman and I inhaled salami, liverwurst, potato salad and tea. Cost eight dollars in groceries to have him join me in watching The Early Show. Two commercials later the set remained hale and hearty but the repairman was sick and nauseous. Seems he's allergic to tea. Exiting, he slammed the door which was all our neurotic set needed. It went on the blink again.

I examined the yellow pages of the Classified and yellowed they were—it was a '49 edition. I located an outfit which listed recommendations from satisfied customers. Satisfied to return to radio, that is. Lump and Schloomp TV Adjustors were endorsed by everybody but Duncan Hines.

I stated we sleep until noon so any time between twelve and five would be convenient. Promptly at nine A.M. their mechanic showed up. My maid hadn't arrived yet. She doesn't even break her first dish until ten-thirty. Soo-o, I dragged my weary carcass out of bed foaming like a stein of Schlitz.

"Lump and Schloomp at your service," he announced.

"Which're you?" I barked.

"I'm a Lump," he said.

You're so right, I thought. He lugged more equipment to fix one busted tube than Ed Murrow's crew used to televise our whole apartment.

He dismantled his tool chest on the floor and he dismantled

my television set on the floor. Everything was removed from inside our set including a 1950 *TV Guide*. He must've screwed the wrong gadgets into the wrong places. All I know is I turned on Channel Four and viewed a close-up of a wrench.

Also, the picture took a long time to focus. He adjusted that. It no longer takes a long time to focus. It now takes only a short time to focus—but it disappears immediately!!

"Probably the antenna on the roof," he decided. "Where's your master?"

"My husband's asleep."

"No," he explained. "I mean the master cable."

"Under the rug."

"Who, your husband?"

"No, the cable."

After he gathered up his gear and left, we didn't have a clearer view of television but we had a clearer view of our living room. You can't have everything. . . . Then our bedroom TV collapsed. No matter how we twirled dials the picture was black. I called in specialists. Held a consultation. I should belong to a TV Blue Cross Plan for what they charged me. Still my picture was black.

Y'know what? One day my maid washed the screen with a damp cloth.

Y'know what else? Now the picture is light again.

Our apartment is currently being painted. The lease guarantees one paint job every three years. This means the painter, pronounced "paintner," dribbles the color of your choice on your furnishings and rugs. If, accidentally, some splatters on the walls this is purely a bonus.

Two days before Operation Housewreck comes in the Boss Paintner. Like all good paintners he has taken the Oath of Sadism. Sporting a pair of overalls from the days when he was an apprentice plasterer, he comes a-calling at eight A.M. Since we retire around six A.M., eight isn't exactly our wake-up time. Even at my tender years one and a half hours isn't considered a night's rest. At my husband's advanced age, it's scarcely more'n a yawn.

I wouldn't say my eyes were dragging but I distinctly recall standing on my lower lid as the Boss Paintner and I amicably discussed what he positively wouldn't do. . . . I wanted one tiny kitchen wallpapered. This he couldn't do. I have to hire a union wallpaper. I wanted my two air conditioners painted the same as the walls. Paintners spill more paint than they'd need for the conditioner and they paint items nobody wants painted. Items like rugs and windows, so I figured they'd oblige by painting something somebody wanted painted for a change. No, this he couldn't do because "Air conditioners don't get painted, they get sprayed," he said. "So, spray it," I said. "Can't. Gotta hire a union sprayer," he said. Holes require union plasterers, the rim of the window molding requires an *outdoor* union paintner and to whisk an ashtray out of the line of paint calls for a union furniture mover. Paintners only paint. If a Rembrandt is hanging on a nail he'll paint over it. They don't look from left to right. Whatever's in front of them gets painted—not removed!

One dark day he was painting an arm instead of the window sill. "Make a light," I said.

"Can't," he said. "Y'gotta hire a union electrician."

The decorator, my husband and I gathered 'round the Boss Paintner at eight A.M. This much attention he never received in his own home. We explained this was to be off-white. Halfway between oyster white and eggshell but definitely not yellow. No creamy tone.

He said nothing but I could tell he was alive. I saw him breathing.

This other room was to be a clear sunny yellow. Not lemony, but yellowy like whipped butter—unsalted. Not orangeyish.

Nothing from the paintner. Not even a twitch from his immobile cigar. The fixed look of death was already upon his lime-green brow.

This wall is to be a bright red, we explained. No cherry or coral or maroon. A clear lipstick, fire-engine type red. We placed three sample swatches on the table.

The resuscitated paintner honored us with a turpentiny belch, strode out ignoring the sample swatches and bellowed to his assistant, "White, yellow and red."

Two mornings later at eight sharp a staff of one worker showed. Never did I think paint could be noisy. It wasn't. He was. The ladder fell. He fell. The paint can fell. When he plastered it was with a vengeance. Korea wasn't this noisy. He knocked and scraped and pounded so vociferously that sympathetic holes began appearing in other walls. As day faded into day, week into month and summer into winter I despaired of ever living sans The Paintner. I made plans to print napkins saying, JOEY, CINDY & THE PAINTNER.

Suddenly, relations between the paintner and the paintee (of which I am she) became strained. I made the mistake of uttering the dreaded words "extra coat." You may use the word "extra" and the word "coat" separately with all safety ... but never put them together in front of a paintner. If your wall is black and you want it white you get one coat. If you say "I want an extra coat" he will blanch, foam, twitch and lie rigid. Then nothing save a hypodermic and a sawbuck (and if you got a sawbuck you can forget the hypo) will neutralize his fit.

Since I only parted with a fin I decided to double up heavy on conversation. So I said to this important individual, I said, "Guess you like meeting celebrities like Joey, don't you?" I said.

"Las' week I done Eva Marie Saint's place," he drawled. As I paled to the off-white of the walls, he added the clincher, "She's a Oscar winner, y' know." Joey agreed with me that I should have given him a sawbuck.

Mondays must be legal holidays to paintners. Never do they begin a job early in the week so they can finish by Friday. Oh, no. If they do this the painters' union fines them. They always start on Thursday so your house can stay wrecked over the weekend while they lie around their own clean homes.

Finally, when there was nothing left to paint except where it was getting dirty already, the paintner and I exchanged phone numbers preparatory to getting together socially. After two birthdays and an anniversary he left, dragging his pails behind him. That was when my husband said quietly, quote, "I don't like the color . . ."

For thirty-three hours last month I owned a dog. This wasn't a plain, pedigreed pup. Not even an average, dog-a-dozen type thoroughbred. This was a genuine, ordinary mangy dorg. And I loved her.

I weekended in that far-flung continent—Long Island. I'm *très* outdoorsy. I figure anything above Bergdorf's is camping out. The weekend began Friday. For me, it ended Friday. Hours after arrival, sans car or friends, I returned to civilization. I left the suburban ants and worms for the urban roaches and carpet beetles. I mean, even to insects, make mine city-style.

Whelan's drugstore adjoined the depot. I wanted a hot dog —and that's what I got! Only this one walked. She was an abandoned two-week-old pup who sniffed me like we were kin. As the cashier graciously noted, "You got the kind of face dogs like." Before I bit him, I and my hound left. During our exit my dog turned up his nose and leg at the store.

Whelan, which I sentimentally labeled her, shivered when we hit the air. Like any devoted mother, I invaded my luggage and wrapped my child in Mommy's best cashmere. Anybody wanting to buy a cashmere, kindly contact me c/o the Bideawee.

The conductors tried bouncing me at every spot on account of animals aren't permitted with humans. This was somewhat insulting because the animal wasn't visible. She was, however, audible. Her two-inch body had a seven-foot larynx which bayed, cried, growled, yipped and barked to Penn Station. 'Tis said mothers know their own children but I hadn't known mine enough to decide whether she wanted a cafeteria or a comfort station. With the passengers glaring at me, animal-human segregation was sensible because further integration might have proven injurious to my animal. My seat mate either loved dogs or girls because he palmed his address should I decide to pawn Whelan. I took it, since Joey, who was away, doesn't relish pets. The only fur around him is in my coats.

Whelan supped from my larder—crackers, salami, sardines —whatever was around. It was late. Stores were closed and the only dogs that ever came to my cocktail parties relished crackers, salami and sardines.

I secured the bathroom doors, papered the floors, bedded her down and retired—for 30 seconds. My infant missed her mommy or uncle or dogcatcher because she began a ceaseless rock 'n' roll medley. At 3 the neighboring apartment began banging. 4 my phone rang. 5 the house phone buzzed. 6 it was the doorbell. 7 the super. 8 the landlord and 9 I visited the vet. My dog was all right but I was a bloody wreck.

The anteroom held fretful parents with their sick children. "Poor Ronald Wonald has a runny wunny nose." Ronald Wonald, a camel-sized wolfhound, was taking all-purpose 4-way gulps out of my thigh. The vet discovered my daughter had fleas, chills, sores and malnutrition. How she acquired that in two weeks I don't know. The vet dosed, inoculated and de-loused $40 worth. I had a vitamin prescription ($6) and a daily formula with special foods ($7). Such care a husband never got! She'd stop barking if she found her mother, the vet said. With an alarm clock (sound of Momma's heart— $2.95) and an electric pad (Momma's heat—$7.95), stick her onto shredded paper, cover warmly and she'd shaddup. I did. She didn't.

Midnight Joey, unaware of our boarder, called and my spaniel and/or airedale began vocalizing. Even long distance Joey recognizes my voice, so I confessed all. Joey's bark was louder than Whelan's.

Whelan, who should've been named Handyman because of the odd jobs she did round the house, didn't shut her snout all night. Early next day, haggard and worn, I taxied to my seat mate ($2.35) and handed him one free Pet plus the $65 worth of haberdoggery he'd acquired.

Oh, well, for thirty-three hours last month I owned a dog. . . .

I love movies.

I see anything. I even go when I can't get passes.

However, certain cinematic idiosyncrasies give me a stiff pain in my loge. F'rinstance, the cowboy stars who have knockdown, drag-out fights. They're whipped, tripped, raced, chased, smashed and bashed. They lose their cattle, their ranches, their guns, their girls . . . but never their hats! Must be when a cowpoke gets barmitzvah'd he goes through a ritual; they nail a five-gallon hat onto him which gains one gallon every birthday until the kid owns a ten-gallon hat at eighteen. From then on he and the hat are together for richer for poorer, in sickness and health, until a bullet do 'em part.

I am also a despiser of the He-Man type who singlehandedly sabotages forty Nazi supply dumps—or was it forty dumpy sloppy Nazis? Anyway, this hero what in real life couldn't handle a sauerbraten alone is shot and beaten. The enemy uses his head as a bowling ball, stuffs an atom bomb up his nostril, kicks him, stabs him and play mumblety-peg with his features until his face looks like chopped liver—next scene he's wearing one skinny Band-Aid on his temple.

I further hate, abhor and am not fond of the heroine who before saying nighty-night swallows eighty Ny-tols, some instant opium and a vat of gin. She's so dead asleep she's getting messages from the spirit world. Next morning when the hero awakens her she flashes more warpaint than Geronimo when he's cranky. Her eyelashes are out to here, her coiffeur's coifed to there and the lipstick is perfect. Either she's a slob who doesn't wash before retiring or she walks in her sleep!

Another thing: in every picture the night club bosses are tough guys. Come to think of it, they are too.

Then there's the Secret Agent who's secretly smuggling

secrets under his hangnail. He's secretly sought by even Se-
creter Foreign Agents because he alone carries the secret JA-4
equation (which nobody but the audience knows is the secret
Lestoil Formula). He sneaks about skulking and lurking—
always in an unbelted trench coat with his forelock over his
eyebrow. Belted trench coats and combed forelocks automati-
cally cancel your Secret Agent union card. At 4:05, in Wee-
hawken, he's warned to amscray. At 4:15, in Idlewild, he's
aboard a plane bound for Lisbon—it's always bound for Lisbon—with no passport, luggage, money, toothbrush or Portu-
guese-American dictionary. All I can say is good luck to him.
I prepare for six months just for a weekend at Grossinger's.

Films about traveling gas me. The star knows beans about
language, customs and currency exchange yet first day abroad
he hits a store where nobody savvys English. Unperturbed he
requests a cherry-red satin overcoat with leopard thingama-
bobs, size 6Z . . . and gets it! Then the salesgirl mumbles in
Aramaic, "That'll be sixty klipchiks, four and a half croips
and a zoog, buster." Without counting, looking or translating
into dollars he plops down the exact amount of dirty leaves
plus a half inch of tinkling Willkie buttons and he's off. This
even Ripley couldn't do.

Why can't outlaws strut into saloons, plunk down a coin
and say "Seltzer"? Why must they always say "Whisky"? No
matter who saunters in, everybody guzzles from one bottle.
Maybe it's shellac. Nobody wants Bell's Twelve, VSOP or
Hennessy Two Star. (It's really Five Star but the picture
doesn't rate more.) All they want is whisky and nobody asks
how much it costs. Everybody leaves one thin coin. Never
more. And nobody ever gets change. I've heard of price stabili-
zation but that's ridiculous.

And howcum bad men shoot and shoot and shoot and never
reload? And howcum the good men can plug a penny in a
man's hand from two states away, blindfolded, at night, up-
side down, while drunk . . . but one poor soul on a lame horse
they miss? And why when the sexpot rides in an open car her
hair never blows?

I wrote Hollywood offering them the benefit of my opinions. Joey said they wouldn't answer me. But they did. They revoked my passes.

I'm addicted to a drug more habit-forming than anything known to medical science. It's called the Late Show. This has only one antidote, the Late Late Show. If I'm out around eleven P.M. I experience hot flashes. Toward eleven-five I perspire freely. At ten past I tremble visibly. If I'm not home within four minutes I undergo Late-Showitis shock.

Never do I okay an engagement without first checking the Late and the Late Late listings. I allocate my friends definite visiting hours—like a clinic. I see them from eight to eleven. No matter where I am, like Cindyrella, I amscray by the witching hour. Whether I'm at a formal soiree, on a triple schneid or in the middle of a movie, I exit by eleven. Not a pal in the world, be he doctor, lawyer, or Indian chief, can compete with Gable, Grable, Harlow and the ever-popular Mae Busch.

By eleven-fourteen I've doffed my glad rags and donned my Late Show ensemble—pajamas, robe, slippers and cold cream. My husband also wears pajamas, robe, slippers, but he doesn't apply his cold cream until the Late Late Show.

This habit has one complication. We antagonize our neighbors. Seems we live in a den of early risers. By nine o'clock everybody in the building is asleep . . . including the doorman. We disturb nobody when Channel Two schedules a love story. However, the other two A.M. John Gilbert dynamited Marie Dressler in a noisy attempt to capture Wally Reid's Stutz Bearcat. This deafening '32 epic was a lullaby compared to our landlord's buzzing and banging. Unfortunately he dwells directly beneath us. His bedtime is our dinnertime, so he hates us from the Early Show yet. Frankly I suspect he's the insomniac who wakes Garroway. Anyway, the following day we received two subpoenas, a dispossess, a frosty glare from the super and the elevator man snubbed us.

Now with the nightly TV debuts in line with CBS's Fabulous February and Magic in March policies we never miss a night, consequently Herr Landlord is a hefty problem. Cowboy films he complains about on account of he can't sleep because of the noise. Tender romances he complains about on account of he can't sleep because it's too quiet and he's waiting for the noise. Recently, halfway through a whodunnit, he complained he couldn't sleep because of the shooting. We shifted our base of operations from the bedroom to the living room. Minutes later he complained again that he couldn't sleep because he had to know whodunnit. We told him the tenant did it.

Late Show fanatics are easily identifiable by their haggard looks and strawberry-like eyeballs. If you meet one early in the evening he will act natural enough. Toward midnight when he begins twitching just spin him around three times and point him in the direction of *TV Guide*. Immediately he hears the rhythm of the syncopated clock, his breathing will become normal and the spasm will cease. Addressing a Late Shownik except during commercials is accomplished at one's own risk. Unnecessary conversation during the movie often results in violence. News of any type must be summarized in the one-minute Roto-rooter spiel. I know one fellow whose wife stuttered and if she hadn't arranged to have the information flashed on the screen, he might never have known he won the Irish Sweepstakes.

Movie habitués suffer from by-products even more discomfiting than the original malady: obesity. At every commercial I run like crazy to gas up so's I can exist through the following quarter-hour segment. Comes the next break I eat my way through the refrigerator again. My brain knows I just gorged myself fifteen minutes before, but my stomach doesn't. I figure television's a desert and the sponsor is an oasis and them as what don't stuff their fat faces ain't gonna last through the vigil.

I don't need a diet to lose weight. I just need to break my TV set.

Rumor says NBC is adding a movie to follow Jack Paar.

My only worry is how'm I gonna watch CBS's Late Late Show and NBC's Terribly Terribly Tardy Show at the same time? And if I do, will it run into the Early Early Show?

I enjoy opera, but I prefer rock 'n' roll, Spike Jones and my own bubblebath monotone—so what do I know. My husband, who's very low on couth, attends the opera whether he needs the sleep or not, but he appreciates good music and to prove it he buys every record Ella Fitzgerald makes. To Joey, opera's Italian vaudeville. He says it's where a man gets stabbed and instead of bleeding he sings. At Chez Adams mail from the Metropolitan means we're behind on our premiums. In other words, a season box we ain't got.

Recently some long-haired friends conned us into *La Traviata*. They were so longhair even the husband had a ponytail. They wore evening clothes, diamonds, high hat and tails —and this was a matinee. Immediately I changed my orlon dress with the matching raincoat and off we went in their '38 Packard. "Only nouveau riche get nouveau cars yearly," they explained.

They piled a libretto, opera glasses with a case and another program thing on me and coupled with my bag, corsage and gloves I spent the first act studying the floor not the stage. While people were applauding and hollering "Bravo," I was retrieving and whispering, "Y' mind lifting your foot, sir?"

Traviata, the consumptive invalid, was lustily executed by a 350-pound soprano who, were she dying, it would be from overweight. At one point this pallid flower, wasted away to a mere ton, collapses in the arms of her lover. Three stagehands were needed to break the fall.

In *Camille*, the movie version, anemic Garbo languidly flutters her lids and swoons onto Robert Taylor's bosom. I blubbered into my popcorn I was so touched. Meanwhile, back at the Met, this weightlifter hoisted herself onto a reinforced chaise and, like an air-raid siren, squawked her death aria to a squat tenor whose pants were too short, too tight and not squat where he was. Only thing believable was her aria. It was real death.

Between acts there's Sherry's. Sherry's is like a sardine can, only here the fish aren't swimming in oil, they're handing it out. The Somebodys get tables. Nobodys try joining Somebodys. The smoke is thick, the conversation worse and the coffee isn't even as hot as the conversation. Everybody's looking at the Duck and Duckling who're ignoring each other craning toward Hollywood's latest Miss Mammary Gland who's eying a Broadway producer who's ogling possible angels. Intermittently, some manufacturer remembers what he's there for and announces "The Mezzo's vibrato reprised to forte on her tremolo" and us peasants what don't know Madame Butterfly from a cocoon are impressed.

Opera audiences don't respond on their own, but when they're shown. "When in Rome do as the clacques do." You cluck when the clacques clacque and anyone bravo-ing solo is considered persona au gratin. Did I know???! I know when Joey works I'm supposed to hustle applause. So, natch, I was the only one clapping in The Horseshoe and I really made a horse's shoe out of myself.

During one scene my friend with the long hair (on her face) mumbled, "How'd you like Madame's fiery cadenza?" Sez I, "Personally I dug her green Balenciaga."

We sat in a box. I'd rather crouch on an orange crate in the orchestra. The box's front row is dandy, but I won the back row and had an exceptional view—of the cyst on the neck of the cornball in front. Only time I saw the stage was at intermission. It was interesting, though. Whenever the soprano sopranoed E over high C the node pulsated. The binoculars were helpful, too. When my arms weren't numb from lifting them I focused on an exceptional enlargement of this friend's dandruff. I wouldn't mind seeing nothing if only I could've heard nothing as well. Mine was the position of a listener hearing opera over radio without the advantage of turning it down.

Somewhere between the overture's downbeat and page three of the libretto, Joey conked out and slept louder than the music. He awoke to the baritone's booming bellow and my crashing elbow. To our hosts' "Howja like *Traviata*?" Joey yawned, "He never sounded better." 'Twas with a song in my heart if not in my ears that the curtain rang down.

I think our hosts got the picture because the next time they invited us anywhere it was to the fights.